Here's what people are saying about *World-Changing Generosity*:

"*World-Changing Generosity* nails it. It is chock full of inspiring true stories of common Joes who have made a difference by living lives of simple yet commanding generosity. This tool has reignited a fire within me to be more generous with my own resources and experience the joy that accompanies audacious generosity."

— Matt Hartsell, founder and executive director, Forgotten Children Worldwide

"This book is not what I expected, nor will it be what you expect. It is a well-researched, enjoyable read on the principles of giving and why we can and should give of ourselves. This is a fantastic, well-written book to guide you on a more fulfilling life. It is full of inspirational anecdotal stories. Jim and Nancy outline the spiritual and even physiologic benefits of giving. With their help, you may master the art of giving and discover how selfish you can be while helping others."

— Dr. Chuck Dietzen, founder and president, Timmy Global Health

"Jim and Nancy Cotterill have given the world a great gift in this thoughtful, helpful, and significant book, *World Changing Generosity*. They provide a historical and religious context, a guide for making good decisions, and powerful insight into the role that philanthropy can play in making the world a better place."

— James T. Morris, Former Executive Director of the United Nations World Food Programme

"The Cotterills provide inspiration to all of us on the journey toward generous giving and generous living. The stories they tell and the insights they bring will lead you to consider how you can be a part of a movement to change the world."

— David P. King, Ph.D., Karen Lake Buttrey Director, Lake Institute on Faith and Giving, Lilly Family School of Philanthropy Indiana University

"Generosity has changed my life as I have both given and received. Generosity has transformational power that cannot be actualized until we fully engage. Jim and Nancy Cotterill's invitation to be a "world-changer" will not just change the world, but our own hearts and lives as well. Beyond inspiring us, the Cotterills give practical tools to begin and sustain this journey into a generous lifestyle."

— Adam Nevins, Executive Director, ServLife International

"There is joy and fulfillment in being generous. This book leads the way in helping all of us ordinary people make an extraordinary difference. Drawing from their personal experiences with giving, Jim and Nancy provide in this book encouragement, education, and inspiration for those desiring to follow the life-changing journey of generosity."

— Wesley K. Willmer, author of *God and Your Stuff*, editor of *Revolution in Generosity*

"Jim and Nancy Cotterill have produced an outstanding resource that encourages everyone—of any religious tradition or of no religious tradition—to enjoy the benefits that come to anyone who gives generously to make a positive difference in the world. I often found myself with tears in my eyes as I read their powerful illustrations of people who live generous lives. Once you start reading it, you won't want to put it down."

— Dr. M. Kent Millard, gratitude coach, Indiana Annual Conference, United Methodist Church

WORLD-CHANGING
GENEROSITY

HOW YOU CAN JOIN THE MOVEMENT OF ORDINARY PEOPLE
MAKING AN EXTRAORDINARY DIFFERENCE FOR THOSE IN NEED

Jim and Nancy Cotterill

WORLD-CHANGING GENEROSITY
HOW YOU CAN JOIN THE MOVEMENT OF ORDINARY PEOPLE MAKING AN EXTRAORDINARY DIFFERENCE FOR THOSE IN NEED

iUniverse books may be ordered through booksellers or by contacting:

iUniverse
1663 Liberty Drive
Bloomington, IN 47403
www.iuniverse.com
1-800-Authors (1-800-288-4677)

ISBN: 978-1-4917-7078-8 (sc)
ISBN: 978-1-4917-7079-5(e)

Library of Congress Control Number: 2015913888

Print information available on the last page.

iUniverse rev. date: 9/22/2015

CONTENTS

PART I: DO WHAT YOU CAN

PART II: STEPPING UP

PART III: GENEROSITY AS A VALUE

PART IV: HOW WORLD CHANGERS GIVE

ABOUT THE AUTHORS

For the last eight years, coauthor Jim Cotterill has served as president of the Indiana arm of the fifteenth-largest public charity in the US, counseling high-capacity donors regarding why to give, how to give, what to give, and where to give. During that time, he has overseen the receipt of more than $185 million in contributions that constantly flow out to support local and international charities. Jim has a passion for transforming our consumer culture into one of generosity by helping individuals join him in an understanding of our place in the world economy and the responsibility we share to live lives that reflect our comprehension of human need. Jim is often called upon to work with business leaders to develop a generous culture in their places of work—the next step in truly changing our culture from one of *getting* to one of *giving*.

Leading a not-for-profit that she founded, coauthor Nancy Cotterill spent more than a decade serving the physically disabled throughout the country. During that time, she developed an online news portal that became a chief source of information for our nation's wheelchair users, raised all operating funds, and conducted annual awards events. Prior to founding this charity, Nancy spent twenty-five years in writing and publishing, as an award-winning editor and editorial writer who served as editorial director with a chain of business newspapers, publisher and editor of a weekly business journal and editor of two monthly business magazines and a monthly consumer magazine.

The authors have served on multiple not-for-profit boards, and they enjoy sharing their time, talent and assets to help those in need. Building upon their personal commitments to lead generous lives and adding to their own life experiences, they have spent the last two years researching the latest information about better ways to give, as well as ways we can all have a hand in addressing the world's deepest needs in the most effective and impactful ways.

Illustrating these precepts with stories of ordinary people who are making an extraordinary difference in the world demonstrates one person's power in the world. On a group level, the tenets of generosity in the top-ten religious and nonreligious groups in the US that are shared this book provide clear proof of the roots we all share in our concepts of and commitment to generous living.

We dedicate this book to the most loving and
generous people we have ever known,
our parents:

Lew and Marge Cotterill
and
Al and Lucile Heppner
and to
Grandpa Abe Glazier.

Your legacy lives on.

ACKNOWLEDGMENTS

Many thanks to Sally Mayhill, Adam Nevins, and Chris Cotterill. We greatly appreciate your help and encouragement during the creation of this work.

Generosity begins at the crossroads where your deep joys and passions intersect with the world's deep needs, blessing you with the opportunity to live life graciously and with integrity.

—Frederick Bueckner (1926–), American writer and theologian

FOREWORD

James T. Morris, former executive director of the United Nations World Food Programme

Jim and Nancy Cotterill have given the world a great gift in their thoughtful, helpful, and significant book, *World-Changing Generosity*. They provide a historical and religious context, a guide for making good decisions, and powerful insight into the role that philanthropy can play in making the world a better place.

The book illustrates that generosity is fundamental to all of the world's great faiths. Whatever our religious beliefs may be, we all share a common commitment to loving our neighbor, caring for our neighbor, and sharing what we have for the well-being of others, with a special emphasis on taking care of at-risk children.

JAMES T. MORRIS

I love the notion of world-changing generosity. Generosity implies not only the sharing and giving of money but the use of one's time, talent, and spirit for others. One of my favorite verses in the New Testament Scriptures is from I John, Chapter 4, verse 20. The question is asked, "If a man say, I love God, and hateth his brother, he is a liar; for he that loveth not his brother whom he hath seen, how can he love God whom he hath not seen?" Our individual lives only take on definition and meaning as we express our concern and love for one another. An act of giving is an act of love.

Mother Teresa reminds us that we are only capable of small acts of love and that we are well advised to begin our charity with the folks with whom we are the closest. She also reminds us that if we don't have peace in the world, it is because we have forgotten that we belong to each other.

How can we as good-hearted, faithful human beings change the world and continue to make substantial progress in reducing the evils and challenges we face? Those who give find a way to make a difference, to become a part of a collegial group who share common passion; they are examples for their children, their families, and those around them and receive enormous satisfaction from being participating, giving individuals. Those who give are happier folks.

This book is both a spiritual and practical handbook and shares the wisdom of all of the great faiths and extraordinary people, such as Mother Teresa, Margaret Meade, the Dali Lama, Elton Trueblood, Gandhi, Paul Farmer, and Benjamin Franklin. There is so much material here and so much to think about. Their work reminds me of the writing of Robert Greenleaf, an extraordinary Hoosier from Terre Haute, Indiana, who rose to senior leadership at AT&T. He was very thoughtful about the use of his time after age sixty. He concluded that he wanted to write and think about issues related to trust, stewardship, and servant leadership. He often said that life was about "the more able and the less able taking care of each other and each becoming healthier, wiser, and freer in the process." One individual personally caring for another is just as important as the sharing of resources.

There are many examples of individuals or institutions doing remarkable things that demonstrate world-changing generosity. There is the example of the Rotary coming very close to eliminating polio in the world and that of local Rotary clubs coming together to honor the memory of the Hoosier poet James Whitcomb Riley for creating one of the greatest children's hospitals in the world, or the Indiana cub scout who raised thousands of dollars to provide protective vests for people in law enforcement.

A brilliant young student, George Srour built a national organization called Building Tomorrow that raised money campus by campus and engaged their school communities in building more than forty schools for children in Uganda. Peter Bakker, CEO of the Dutch Company TNT, was overcome by the problem of world hunger. He asked himself what he was going to do about it and made the resources of his extraordinary company available to the World Food Programme, greatly enhancing WFP and, in the process, he changed the culture of his own company.

Carl Stern, CEO of the Boston Consulting Group, did much the same thing. There's the example of Jeff Simmons and Elanco using all of the company's strength in animal health to address world hunger and to engage their colleagues in the effort that has influenced numerous companies and affected hundreds of thousands of vulnerable people. There are also examples of members of a wide range of religions coming together to address child hunger in their hometowns.

The power of a brilliant young lady, Tamika Catchings, playing basketball for the Indiana Fever; her spirit has changed the lives of thousands of Indiana young people through her generosity and concern for their well-being. Our own city of Indianapolis has been transformed through the generosity of incredible families and more than one hundred and twenty companies that contributed between 2 and 5 percent of pretax profits for the development of their hometown.

I spent five years as the director of the UN World Food Programme, the largest humanitarian agency in the world. The lessons learned there about generosity were powerful. When people were aware of a crisis, money would flow in. Most of the world's hungry were out of sight of news coverage, and those dollars were more difficult to raise. Through a brilliant partnership led by Senators George McGovern and Robert Dole and supported by countries all over the world, we were able to feed a hungry child in school for nineteen cents per day, or thirty-five dollars per school year. This dramatically changed everything about their individual lives and their communities. So little goes so far. What a difference the generous soul can make. How rewarding and affirming giving can be for each and all.

I am grateful to Jim and Nancy for telling the story and laying out the pathway and for their willingness to personalize their own journey, as they understand the profound relationship between faith and generosity. This book will touch, inspire, encourage, inform, and motivate each reader who takes the time to think about the significance and opportunity each of us has to make a difference. Thanks to the Cotterills for their passion and wisdom and giving us so much to think about.

Thank God for faith, family, friends, community, and vocation and for the opportunity to change the world through generosity.

ABOUT JAMES T. MORRIS

James T. Morris served as the tenth executive director of the United Nations World Food Programme from April 2002 to April 2007.

In July 2002, Mr. Morris was appointed UN Secretary-General Kofi Annan's special envoy for Humanitarian Needs in Southern Africa, a region that continues to be gripped by a major food emergency. In 2003, he successfully guided WFP in carrying out the largest humanitarian operation in history, feeding twenty-six million Iraqis.

Prior to leading WFP, Mr. Morris combined a distinguished career of business, philanthropic, and humanitarian leadership with a personal life of public service. Both his career and his voluntary activities have always reflected a commitment to improving the lives of others, with a special interest in at-risk young people and in giving something back to his city, his country, and the international community.

WHAT THE WORLD NEEDS RIGHT NOW

People were created to be loved. Things were created to be used. The reason the world is in chaos is because things are being loved, and people are being used.

—Unknown

For the most part, Americans are insulated from the constant drama that encompasses the lives of people in much of the rest of the world. In a place where most people never miss a meal, it is easy to forget that for those without food, there is only desperation—every day, all the time.

Hunger is like that, which is probably why food, a basic physiological need, is at the foundation of Maslow's hierarchy of needs. Safety is right above it. Once your stomach is full, having a safe place to sleep becomes very important. When people have no roof over their heads at night and when they or their children are sick and there is nowhere to turn, every day is a war against the inevitable dangers that spring from the root of poverty. These people include the homeless on the street and the runaway kids under the bridge. They live in the Sudan and in St. Louis, Minneapolis, and Mumbai.

There are other needs as well. Maybe it is temporary, like a town cleaning up after a tornado. Maybe the need is across the globe, or maybe it is just across the street. The job can be as basic as feeding people or as complicated as providing educational opportunities that will allow them to provide for themselves and their families over generations.

While there are lots of problems, there are also plenty of us to solve them. The job of changing the world will require *many* people to care. This book is a first step—a short course in some of the amazing people around us who make a difference in the world and the critical needs that they address. You'll quickly understand that there is a need for you to find that place where *your* energy can change a life ... where you can be amazing too.

We have written not only about people who are generous, why people are generous, and how to be generous, but also about how major US religious and nonreligious groups address generosity.

For many, the fact that their belief system promotes and even demands generosity on behalf of believers may come as a surprise. And while it is impossible to claim generosity as the property of a single religion or group, in our personal faith, we believe that all people are created in God's image, and that we are to love and encourage everyone of every color and belief, no matter where they live. For this reason, we have included the generosity tenets of most of the US population in part III. Each group has strong tenets of generosity, and every one claims tens of thousands—and in some cases, millions—of followers. This book has been written to encourage everyone to step shoulder to shoulder into this movement, to do something to change the world.

From the seven-year-old boy who played a harmonica to raise money to provide healing for children in Africa to the man who engineered wheelchairs out of plastic lawn chairs for the world's physically disabled population, there's a legacy that belongs to you and you alone. This book can inspire you to find it, and we hope you'll find it soon.

Believe it or not, we occupy a critical moment in history when, with enough input, we actually could solve some of the most critical problems of the world. Sounds like a fantasy, but you'll see that according to some unimpeachable experts, you really could be one of the people who leaves this world a better place.

You don't have to quit your job or school. The World-Changing Generosity movement is something that everyone can take part in with the time and energy they have. It's not political or commercial. It's not a club, and there are no dues. Rather, this book and the idea of the movement are about the flowering of the individual reader in ways that benefit him- or herself while making the world a better place.

In our research, we kept encountering columns and stories quoting Stephen King, the famous American author of contemporary horror and suspense, who spoke powerfully on the subject of generosity in a speech he made to graduates of Vassar College a few years ago. As an introduction to the thought process we endorse, his statements are invaluable.

So here is Steve King, as he calls himself, on a subject that has nothing to do with horror. In fact, it is a recipe for a happy life, well lived, from a man whose life-threatening experience mirrors one of our own (see The Prequel).

AUTHOR STEPHEN KING

A couple of years ago I found out what "you can't take it with you" means. I found out while I was lying in a ditch at the side of a country road, covered with mud and blood and with the tibia of my right leg poking out the side of my jeans like a branch of a tree taken down in a thunderstorm. I had a MasterCard in my wallet, but when you're lying in a ditch with broken glass in your hair, no one accepts MasterCard.

We come in naked and broke. We may be dressed when we go out, but we're just as broke. Warren Buffet? Going to go out broke. Bill Gates? Going out broke. Tom Hanks? Going out broke. Steve King? Broke. Not a crying dime.

All the money you earn, all the stocks you buy, all the mutual funds you trade—all of that is mostly smoke and mirrors. It's still going to be a quarter-past getting late whether you tell the time on a Timex or a Rolex.

So I want you to consider making your life one long gift to others. And why not? All you have is on loan, anyway. All that lasts is what you pass on.

Now imagine a nice little backyard, surrounded by a board fence. Dad—a pleasant fellow, a little plump—is tending the barbecue. Mom and the kids are setting the picnic table: fried chicken, coleslaw, potato salad, a chocolate cake for dessert. And standing around the fence, looking in, are emaciated men and women, starving children. They are silent. They only watch.

That family at the picnic is us; that backyard is America, and those hungry people on the other side of the fence, watching us sit down to eat, include far too much of the rest of the world: Asia and the subcontinent; countries in Central Europe, where people live on the edge from one harvest to the next; South America, where they're burning down the rain forests; and most of all, Africa, where AIDS is pandemic and starvation is a fact of life.

It's not a pretty picture, but we have the power to help, the power to change. And why should we refuse? Because we're going to take it with us? Please.

Giving isn't about the receiver or the gift but the giver. It's for the giver. One doesn't open one's wallet to improve the world, although it's nice when that happens; one does it to improve one's self.

A life of giving—not just money, but time and spirit—repays. It helps us remember that we may be going out broke, but right now we're doing O.K. Right now we have the power to do great good for others and for ourselves.

So I ask you to begin giving, and to continue as you begin. I think you'll find in the end that you got far more than you ever had, and did more good than you ever dreamed.

—Stephen King

PART I: DO WHAT YOU CAN

Practicing the sacred art of giving helps replace the narrow perspective of "me" with an expansive view of "we."

—LAUREN TYLER WRIGHT,
AUTHOR OF *GIVING — THE SACRED ART*

CHAPTER ONE

THE POWER OF ONE: CHANGING THE WORLD – ONE GIVER AND ONE RECIPIENT AT A TIME

Never worry about numbers. Help one person at a time, and always start with the person nearest you.

—MOTHER TERESA

Many years ago, there was a writer who used to go to the ocean to do his work. He had a habit of walking on the beach before he began writing.

One day, as he was walking along the shore, he looked down the beach and saw a human figure moving like a dancer. He smiled to himself at the thought of someone who would dance to the day, and so he walked faster to catch up.

As he got closer, he noticed that it was a young man and that he was not dancing at all. The young man was reaching down to the sand, picking up small objects, and throwing them into the ocean.

The writer came closer still and called out, "Good morning! May I ask what you are doing?"

The young man paused, looked up, and replied, "Throwing starfish into the ocean."

"Why are you throwing starfish into the ocean?" asked the writer.

To this the young man replied, "The sun is up and the tide is going out. If I don't throw them in, they'll die."

"But young man," said the writer, "don't you realize that there are miles and miles of beach and starfish all along every mile? You can't possibly make a difference."

At this, the young man bent down, picked up yet another starfish, and threw it into the ocean. As it met the water, he said, "It made a difference to that one."

This famous story has been told and retold so many times that it may be familiar to you. But its meaning brings home the critical point that every single individual life is worth extraordinary effort. It introduces us to the hero who is simply doing what he can. That's what *World-Changing Generosity* is all about—each of us simply doing what we can.

A LONE STARFISH ON THE BEACH

Throughout this book, you will be introduced to men, women, and even young children who did what came naturally to them: living normal lives that include radical ideas of sharing and caring about others. People next door, people they came across in their work, and people around the world were saved, cured, and uplifted because these people had an idea and they did what they could do.

Their acts were as simple as buying a hamburger for a homeless man or as complex as challenging a foreign country's legal system to free slaves; each act of generosity started as a nudge, a thought, an urge to do something that they were capable of doing.

When seeing someone in need, each of us has felt the inner challenge to help, but we often stifle the impulse. A few years ago, Phil Collins wrote a song called "Another Day in Paradise" that dealt with those same feelings.

In the song, a young woman is asking for help, calling out to a man as he stands on the side of a street. She has nowhere to stay for the night, and she asks him if he knows of a place where she can stay. The words of the song reflect, perhaps, our own reactions when faced with a similar situation.

> *He walks on, doesn't look back, He pretends he*
> *can't hear her*
> *Starts to whistle as he crosses the street, Seems*
> *embarrassed to be there.*

And off he goes. You can just see him, feeling pressured, not knowing what to do. In most cases we are simply unaware of our own power in such a situation. To the homeless, we are the people with those magic keys that unlock the doors to a safe place to sleep at night—we must have information that can help, they think. Maybe we do. Maybe we can.

Sarah's Plan

At eleven thirty in the morning, Sarah McMullen* was searching among letters she'd received from her readers for another subject for her advice column. Her husband's business had taken a nosedive, cutting his income in half, and she had been laid off from her job as a newspaper reporter. But luckily, Sarah had managed to get a freelance job writing an advice column for a nearby suburban newspaper. It didn't pay much—just pennies a word—but even a little extra money would help bridge the gap.

After a month of work, she'd received a check for $500, which she cashed, putting the money aside to pay for groceries, the kids' lunches, and anything else they needed for the month. Then she opened the letter that changed her plans.

It read:

> I read your article about how to get ready for the holidays. So let me tell you about my holiday plans. My husband got laid off a year ago and can't find work. He walks around the house all day in a depression so deep he barely speaks. My son is autistic. Not the kind that does brilliant math problems in his head, the kind that is belligerent and mean. We have a full-fledged war every morning just getting him dressed and to school. The power company says it will turn the lights off if we don't pay the bill, and I don't have the money to pay the bill. We have nothing in the house to eat but some canned beans, and I don't know how long the water company will keep the water on without me paying them. I could go on, but it would do no good. To say we will have no Christmas goes without saying. Right now we have no future either.

Sarah stared at the letter she held in her hand. She looked over at the ten $50 bills on her desk and at the woman's return address on the envelope.

The next day, Sarah's high school–aged children delivered the money to the woman, posing as volunteers from a charitable group. They knocked on the door, made a quick explanation, and handed her the "Christmas" envelope. The woman's eyes opened wide and filled with tears as she realized what she was receiving. She was overwhelmed, dumbstruck. Shaking, smiling, her whole body seemed to glow with gratitude as she looked from one teenager to the other in an effort to thank them.

Sarah's children were moved too, and they quickly left. They drove home in silence, trying to wrap their minds around what they had witnessed, taking with them a new understanding of the power of generosity and its great blessing, not only in the life of an individual recipient but also in the lives of those who give.

*Name has been changed.

Sarah is a woman with a generous heart. When asked about her gift to this woman—a woman she didn't even know—she has little to say. A common thought of hers is, *They need it more than I do.* However, it was clear that this was a situation in which she wanted to involve her children, knowing it would give them a lesson they would never forget.

Many of us feel we don't really come in contact with people we can help. For those, there are great charitable organizations that do the one-on-one work for us. Sometimes they work in Africa, and sometimes they work around the corner. Most charities always need money.

But sometimes, like Sarah, we get a chance to do the one-on-one work ourselves. Take the lady who was rushing through freezing weather to Walmart to pick up a few things.

Lucky and Tiger

As Audria Roettgen scurried into the Jefferson City, Missouri, Walmart on a freezing January day, she stopped short to see if she could help a homeless man panhandling outside the store, his tiny puppy wrapped in his arms.

The temperature was already dropping into the predicted single digits. As they talked, she noticed he was feeding a sandwich he had been given to the puppy he called Tiger. He told her he was trying to raise enough money to get a hotel room for the night—a hotel that would let him bring in a pet, since homeless shelters don't allow animals.

It was clear he wasn't going to part with his puppy, so within minutes she had arranged for a cab to pick him up and had paid for a two-night stay for the man and his dog at the nearby Baymont Inn & Suites. "My buddy comes first," said Lucky of Tiger. "I'm happy to be here, but as long as I'm able to take care of him, that's the main thing."

The story was picked up by local TV station, KRCG, and immediately went viral. Within hours, people from seven states had contacted the hotel and donated money for Lucky and Tiger to be able to stay for ten nights.

The hotel staff then joined in. Inspired by others' generosity, they wanted to pay it forward and make a donation worth twice what the room cost to a local shelter for the homeless. Hotel management now says all profits from Lucky's stay will also go to a shelter.

A few days later, the hotel reported that donations had reached a point where the pair could stay at the hotel until at least the end of January. Others donated groceries and dog food and paid for veterinary care for Tiger.

The amazing thing about Audria Roettgen is how quickly she acted.

1. The man and his dog will freeze.
2. Call a cab.
3. Get him a room.

Done and done.

May we all react so quickly and so selflessly in the face of need. And maybe you do. Since you're reading this book, very likely you are also following a path toward leading a generous life. In fact, right now, you might be mentally reviewing some of the selfless acts you have performed. And if you are, that's fantastic. Keep going and keep reading. With you, we'll discover more creative with ways to be generous, and we'll help uncover that unfathomable well inside each of us that brings forth great ideas, huge efforts, and incredible, life-saving results.

The stories you have read so far have mainly dealt with individuals who saw a critical need they could personally impact. But larger issues exist that can't be quickly or easily solved. For most of us, the best way to move the needle is to support an organization or two that work in our areas of interest. But one young California man took an amazing journey of generosity that began in the streets of inner-city Los Angeles and took him to the courtrooms of India and China.

Drive-By Caring

Jeff Pankratz, armed with a spanking-new Cal Poly degree in business administration, regularly drove through inner-city Los Angeles to get to his new job. The streets were lined with boarded-up stores, groups of unemployed men, and kids with no one to watch over them. Gang graffiti was scrawled on the walls above sleeping, apparently homeless people. What a contrast to the gleaming office he occupied at a local Fortune 500 company.

Day by day, it became more and more evident to him that merely driving through wasn't going to improve things for those people or do anything to get rid of the ache in his gut that nagged him to somehow help them. So Jeff dove in; he spent years as a volunteer with church-based youth, housing, and civil rights programs. Knowing he needed a stronger platform from which to help, he went back to school and earned a law degree, allowing him to provide much-needed criminal and civil legal aid.

Now married with a family, he and his wife immersed themselves in helping at-risk individuals, living in dangerous neighborhoods with their three daughters in an effort to be close to those they served.

But larger plans beckoned. After almost twenty years of working in the inner city, Jeff was offered an opportunity in Washington, DC. Later he traveled to Asia, where he came face to face with a culture that still tolerated and seemed to ignore the degradation of human beings trapped in modern-day slavery.

In a wholly new way, Jeff was stopped in his tracks. For him, business could not continue as usual. Young girls and women were kept as sex slaves, and families—even whole villages—were enslaved in forced labor, often without the provision of food and always unpaid, treated like animals while the communities around them turned their backs. Jeff's path took an unexpected turn.

He began taking on pro bono legal work aimed at freeing and restoring enslaved people. He quickly found the need so overwhelming and the human deprivation so painful to witness that he moved with his family to India to work on behalf of the hundreds and thousands trapped in forced labor, slavery, and sex trafficking.

JEFF PANKRATZ, CENTER, SURROUNDED BY REPRESENTATIVES FROM JVI'S INDIA TEAM AND ONE OF ITS JUSTICE PARTNERS.

An organization was needed. In 2007, Jeff founded Justice Ventures International with a mission to "secure freedom, justice and restoration for the poor and oppressed." Those are big words. Big words for saving thirteen-year-olds from sex slavery, for taking whole villages out of unpaid forced labor by bringing legal action against owners; big words for profound, life-saving results that affected one person, ten people, three hundred people at a time. Jeff never runs out of people he and his organization can help— and that is world-changing generosity in action.

One man, one family, walked a path that led them to do what they could to help others. They began one on one with the people who were right in front of them and began an effort that has saved lives on the other side of the globe.

The Government's Job

While there are some who excuse themselves from the fight against needs like these by reasoning that generosity is the job of governments, the case for individual involvement is substantial.

When only governments are charged with the distribution of funds and efforts aimed at charitable needs, a powerful interface of caring human contact is lacking. At the same time, political motives often bend charitable efforts to fit partisan aims, altering what should be heart-led efforts of care into politically motivated exercises.

Inherently, governmental agencies carry a great deal of overhead, wasting critical resources that could be going directly to serve the needy. And those in the mission field report the widely accepted view that, in addition to being far more cost-effective than government, charities are superior in the ways they step lightly over barriers to quickly reach those in need.

That's why it is so important that we, as individuals, follow our hearts—and it isn't that hard. We remember a woman who told us she was very worried about children

CITIZENS AGAINST GOVERNMENT WASTE: YOUR INCOME TAX DOLLAR

starving in Africa. She was obsessed with pictures of little ones with bulging stomachs drinking some kind of pasty food out of a gourd.

One of us asked, "Do you support a child in Africa? Or perhaps one of the ten-dollar-a-month food banks that feed people in regions of dire poverty there?"

"No," she said. No, she had never thought of that.

So often, when we hear of an overwhelming problem, our response is, "I'm just one person; there is no way I can fix that." But while we might not be able to fix the overwhelming problem by ourselves, we can throw some seed onto the earth and see what grows from even a small effort. Like the young man in the starfish story, we just have to do what we can do, because each individual life is valuable. And maybe you can save one, if not more.

Police Protection

When Miami-Dade police officer Vicki Thomas was called to deal with a shoplifting case at the local Publix grocery store, she found that the perpetrator was a young mother.

Joblessness had left Jessica Robles without money to feed her children. When Thomas asked Robles why she tried to steal the groceries, she offered no elaborate story. She simply said that her children were hungry.

Thomas asked her, "Do you have *any* food at home?"

The answer: "None at all."

With that, Officer Thomas walked back inside the grocery store and purchased one hundred dollars' worth of food for the family. Her reward was seeing the woman's young sons excitedly rummaging through the loaded grocery bags for food. "It was like Christmas," Thomas said. "That one hundred dollars to me was worth it."

When interviewed, the officer said she knew that arresting this young mother wasn't going to feed her hungry children. "I have done similar things before," she said, "and the people I work with have also done similar things. I was a single mom," said the policewoman. "That could have been me."

Officer Thomas knew what to do in that instant. Her inner voice spoke: "That could have been me." Then she did that thing that generous people do: she put herself in the other person's shoes. The woman had no money and a house full of hungry children. That was the *why* that day in Florida. Just remember that the why is huge. The why is how your effort and energy benefit others. The why is how many lives are saved and many sick people healed. But the why is also what generosity does to you and for you. It is the change in your mindset and heart that takes you to another level on a great big escalator of evolved loving and giving.

> *You have not lived today until you have done something for someone who can never repay you.*
>
> —John Bunyan, 1628–1688, author of The Pilgrim's Progress

As Mother Teresa suggested, help one person at a time and always start with the person nearest you. That's what Jody Richards did.

You Deserve a Break Today

Jody Richards saw a homeless man begging outside McDonald's, so he entered the store and bought the man a cheeseburger. That's not really a big deal. No, it's not, until you realize that Richards is also homeless, and the 99¢ cheeseburger accounted for a substantial percentage of the $9.50 that Richards had earned by panhandling that day.

Albert Lexie also started with the people next to him. This humble family man spent thirty years in a modest profession that yielded a decades-long act of generosity, bringing him not only joy, but marking him as noble in an ignoble world.

Generosity that Shines

Albert Lexie, from Monessen, Pennsylvania, retired after three decades of rising at five thirty in the morning to catch two buses that brought him to his twice-weekly job shining shoes at the Children's Hospital of Pittsburgh. He was so moved by the sick children right there in front of him that he decided to donate his tips to the Children's Hospital Free Care Fund, a charity that provides financial assistance to parents of sick children who can't afford medical costs.

ALBERT LEXIE

A shoe shine costs five dollars, but Lexie said customers had been generous with their tips since he started working at the hospital in 1981. Most customers gave him six dollars; some gave seven, and a doctor gave him a fifty-dollar bill for Christmas once.

Lexie lived on the five-dollars-a-shine budget his whole

working life and saved all of his tips to give away. By the time he retired, Albert Lexie, a man who shined shoes for a living, had contributed more than $200,000 to the Free Care Fund at the Children's Hospital.

Said Greg Barrett, the hospital's foundation president, to the *Pittsburgh Post-Gazette*, "Mr. Lexie is a truly selfless person in every way. It's a great thing for the kids, it's a great thing for the community—the money is great—but the real gift is what Albert represents. I know it sounds like a cliché, but he really does make other people better."

Lexie's personal website tells the story of his efforts for the hospital and its little patients, and it requests tips that continue to go to the fund.

Are those who exercise their generosity muscles somehow different from the rest of us? Albert Lexie is described as "truly selfless" and as a person who "makes other people better." Officer Thomas upholds the law and leads with her heart. Audria Roettgen takes care of business when she sees someone in need. Jeff Pankratz refashions his life to end slavery. The young man in the Starfish story is fictitious. But, like him, there are many among us, otherwise normal folks, who know intimately the power of one, because they do what they can do to help others every day.

CHAPTER TWO

GIVE IT UP!: THE CIRCULAR MOTION OF GIVING AND RECEIVING

You've got to give a little ...
Take a little ...
And let your poor heart break a little ...
That's the story of, that's the glory of, love

—FROM "GLORY OF LOVE"
BY BILLY HILL, SONGWRITER 1899–1940

Mick Jagger and the Rolling Stones—or, if you prefer, some country group—waits in the wings of a giant auditorium. An announcer takes the stage and yells into the microphone: "Give it up for The Rolling Stones!" ... or Toby Keith or Coldplay.

ROLLING STONES' MICK JAGGER
JSTONE / SHUTTERSTOCK.COM

The building rocks with the response of the audience. They whistle, cheer, clap, and whoop out of an overflow of love, energy, and excitement as the artists take the stage. And what follows is a reciprocal outpouring of love, energy, and excitement from the artists to the assembled crowd. If one side drops the ball—if one or the other fails to deliver—the evening is a bust.

Life has patterns. From an airplane, rivers look very similar in design to the very veins that crisscross our bodies; Euclid's triangle is the same shape Canada geese take to cross vast territories in their annual migration; the life cycle of a simple flower, which sprouts, grows, reproduces, flourishes for a time and dies, mimics the life of every human being.

So, too, an evening with the artist on the stage mimics the experience of generosity in our lives. Love is given and returned. What you put out into the world is returned. What goes around comes around. The circular motion of all things is recognized in virtually every study of life and the living. So, what have you been given in the world? And how do you reciprocate?

Circular motion ceases if one only takes and never gives back. If the beach never returns to the sea the deluge that comes in on high tide, it will soon cease to exist because of its greed for seawater. People are no different. We can get so caught up in how much we've amassed in our 401(k)s, IRAs, CDs, and other locations for our stash, we forget that living is taking place now—not only for ourselves but for those in need.

Back to the words of Billy Hill at the beginning of this chapter: "You've got to give a little, take a little, and let your poor heart break a little." For one young girl, what broke her heart—more than a little—were starving orphans in Haiti.

Anna's Story

Anna Lipscomb is a teenager from the Midwest, easily the girl next door in pretty much any middle-class neighborhood in America.

When she was a child, Anna's parents started a family club among their children to encourage them to live generously. As

19

a result, since she was five years old, Anna has been ringing a Salvation Army bell at Christmas time, handing out holiday baskets in the inner city, and giving the birthday presents she received herself to a local city ministry to be regifted to children in need.

ANNA LIPSCOMB WITH CHILDREN IN HAITI

When she was eleven years old, Anna's parents took her on a mission trip to Haiti, where she was struck by the extreme poverty that she witnessed. The water was filthy, there was garbage everywhere, and entire families were living in little shacks and makeshift tents.

But Anna's heart was broken by the children. Orphaned children, as many as eight at a time, literally hung all over her, and although they didn't speak English, they connected with her in a profound way. She realized that thousands of parentless children had been cast adrift in the streets. They were reduced to begging, and most were hungry and without hope. So this determined eleven-year-old decided to try to do something about it.

When she returned home, Anna, somewhat naively, decided that she might be able to raise enough money to build an orphanage in Haiti. At a young age she had learned to play the violin, and she could sing. So she decided to record some songs, make a CD, and sell it to make the money to build her orphanage.

One night, she says, God gave her a song. She wrote it down on sticky notes, amazed and grateful that this music seemed to alight in her mind like a butterfly landing on a shoulder. She called the song, "Heart for Haiti." A year passed, and although she often considered giving up, she persevered, making numerous trips to the recording studio, choosing songs that she could record with her father and others. The CD, called "Anna ... from the Heart" came out two years later, when she was thirteen years old. She began to tell her story, performing and selling her CDs.

Then, in January of 2010, when a massive earthquake devastated Haiti, interest in her project soared and requests for Anna to speak and perform skyrocketed. By the time she was sixteen, Anna had raised $90,000. She has built not one but two orphanages for Haitian orphans through the Global Orphan Project. By the ripe old age of eighteen, she had also partially funded the building of a school and started focusing her fundraising on providing an education for children in this still-impoverished nation. For $180 she can send a child to school for a year. In fall of 2014, 125 children started a school year paid for by Anna's efforts.

It is said that good deeds are not necessarily done by those who are able but by those who are available. Anna made herself available. She did what she could do.

Her concern for the children she encountered in Haiti resulted in a personal act of extreme generosity. A project that started out as an effort to help children on an island a thousand miles away from her hometown resulted in an internal transformation in a young woman who now knows the power that one Midwestern teenage girl can have.

Anna is not rich or poor. She's like most people in the US who have enough food on the table and a safe place to sleep. But wherever you are on the income spectrum, giving produces the growth in inner strength and well-being from the physical change noted by the famous doctor, Dr. Seuss.

> And what happened, then? Well, in Whoville they say—that the Grinch's small heart grew three sizes that day.
>
> —Dr. Seuss, How the Grinch Stole Christmas

What Goes Around

Bighearted givers, like Anna, attest to another circular effect of helping others. Simply put, giving makes them happy. Could it be that Anna and other generous people experience life in a different, more complete, even more joyful way? The answer is yes. In fact, science backs up this assertion.

Americans will spend more than half a billion dollars this year on self-help books, all designed to do one thing: make the reader happier. Whether the books are about diet, finance, marriage, depression, or fitness, readers hope, somehow, that the changes these books inspire will provide, in the end, a more joyful existence.

With that thought in mind, you could be holding in your hands the mother of all self-help books, although you might not have been looking for one. Because if inner peace and happiness are the questions, then giving is the answer—the silver bullet that can help to cure the world's deepest hurts while bringing you perhaps the greatest joy you've ever known.

Researchers have been fascinated by the seemingly contradictory effect that happiness is generated by the act of giving something away. Although most Americans are uncomfortable putting any emphasis on the tie between personal gratification and generosity, a large body of research remains that should not be ignored.

One study, conducted by Jordan Grafman, PhD, director of Brain Injury Research at Rehabilitation Institute of Chicago, found that giving literally lights up the same pleasure centers in the brain that are engaged by sexual activity. Further, the brain's response to giving is far more pleasurable than was documented when study participants merely received a gift. The meaning is clear: we are actually hardwired to give, designed to be generous.

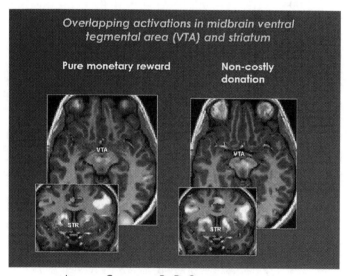

JORDAN GRAFMAN, PHD: CHARITABLE GIVING
LIGHTS UP KEY BRAIN AREAS.

The content of the book *The Paradox of Generosity, Giving We Receive, Grasping We Lose* is based on five years of research conducted through the Science of Generosity Initiative at University of Notre Dame. In its pages, coauthors Christian Smith, PhD, and Hilary Davidson explain that this research regarding the link between generosity and a happier, healthier life involved surveying more than two thousand Americans, as well as in-depth interviews with people throughout the nation.

The results are counterintuitive, which is why Smith and Davidson refer to this as the "paradox of generosity." When we practice giving (a loss of a resource and/or what that resource could have bought), we receive greater well-being—usually something better than we gave: health, happiness, avoidance of depression, and greater purpose in life.

The authors explain that the finding that generous givers are happier people is not only a religious or philosophical teaching but a statistically significant sociological fact. By giving for the well-being of others, we enhance our own lives.

There's more to giving than money. There is also time and talent, as well as lavishing your full attention upon another (relational generosity) and visiting or helping those around you or inviting them to visit you (neighborly generosity). In addition to the positive impact on the giver of money, research shows that the more hours people volunteer, the happier they are; the more people practice relational generosity, the happier they are, and the more they practice neighborly generosity, the happier they are.

Well, Benny is one person who must have realized an immense amount of happiness as a result of his practice of generous giving.

No Ordinary Cereal Box

When Tammy Tompkins opened a box of cereal she had purchased from Walmart, she saw what she thought was a folded up dollar bill.

As she unfolded it, she discovered it was a one-hundred-dollar bill. It was a miracle for Tammy, whose husband's stroke and many hospital stays had left the family mired in debt. She was so happy she cried.

On the back, the bill was signed "Benny" in blue ink, a signature that has become the calling card for a generous and anonymous person who gives away "Bennys," or bills with Benjamin Franklin on them.

He left nine of them on the Boy Scouts' table where they were selling snacks and a trail of bills in other places, touching lives all over Salem, the state capital of Oregon.

$100 BILL, SIGNED BENNY

But Tammy's story didn't end with Benny's one-hundred-dollar bill. When the story was published in the local Statesman Journal, readers were so touched they began to send Tammy donations of their own. The article mentioned that Tammy's husband wanted to use the one hundred dollars to get her wedding ring out of hock, but Tammy felt they needed the money to pay bills.

The couple was able to do both through the generosity of one anonymous person and a host of others who sent money to the Tompkins family. "Benny" and others did what they could and gave a couple in want not only needed funds but the realization that they mattered, that humanity exists to care, and that the needs of two can be as important as the needs of many.

Reading these stories of generosity makes us feel good. But for the givers, the feeling is much more substantial. For them, there is an experience of deep joy, fulfillment, and accomplishment, plus an inner urging to do it again and again.

In one study, authored by Harvard University and the University of British Columbia and released in 2013, researchers found that in terms of quantifying happiness, the act of spending money on oneself barely moves the needle, but spending on others causes a significant increase in the brain areas associated with happiness, further bolstering the concept of a circular relationship in generous living. Meanwhile, cultural analysts have found other benefits to giving that, while anecdotal, occur so often that the evidence has been noticed by researchers.

> In one study, researchers found that in terms of quantifying happiness, the act of spending money on oneself barely moves the needle, but spending on others causes a significant increase in the brain areas associated with happiness.

In 2003, when Arthur C. Brooks, head of a research group in

Washington, DC, was working on a book about charitable giving, he said that he stumbled across what he considered a strange pattern in his data. He found that people who donated money ended up with more income after making their gifts. As he dug more deeply into the information, he found that there was solid evidence that giving stimulated prosperity.

> *My own experience about all the blessings I've had in my life is that the more I give away, the more that comes back. That is the way life works, and that is the way energy works.*
>
> —Kenneth Blanchard, Bestselling author, *The One Minute Manager* and *Who Moved My Cheese*

Brooks says, "I viewed my results as implausible," and he filed the information away. But he shared his findings with a colleague, who encouraged him. Digging deeper, Brooks found that psychologists have long known that donating and volunteering bring many benefits to those who give, and his hypothesis became, "If charity raises well-being, there is no obvious reason it would not also indirectly stimulate material prosperity as people improve their lives."

The story of a young man who was down on his luck is a case in point. He is a Gen-Xer living near San Francisco who, on a very bad day, pursued happiness through generosity. (Or perhaps because of his generosity, happiness pursued him?)

> *If you want others to be happy, practice compassion. If you want to be happy, practice compassion.*
>
> —Dalai Lama

A Lousy Day

Thirty-three-year-old Michael Simas had been recently laid off from his job in the Bay Area of California and had received his final paycheck.

He had moved there from Portland, Oregon, a few years earlier to take care of his ailing father. He eventually took a sales job with a start-up company nearby. But when the company ran short of funding, jobs were cut, and Michael's job was one of them. The day he received his final check was a "lousy day," he said. So he decided to make the day better.

MICHAEL SIMAS

After cashing his check, he stopped at a Taco Bell for something to eat, and he slipped the server a one-hundred-dollar tip. He said, "To see the smile on her face really cheered me up." Next, he walked into a grocery store and requested permission help buy groceries for some of the patrons. The manager, deciding the young man was serious, gave him the okay.

As the store flooded with people in the late afternoon, Michael sought out those who needed some help and gave it. In all, he spent about $600 in the store and donated to the store's food drive. He didn't leave his name.

Locals began calling him the "Mystery Man of Concord, California" until a friend, who describes Simas as having "a beautiful, giving soul" leaked his identity to the area *Concord Costa Times.*

When interviewed, the "Mystery Man" said that the story really began when he was a kid who was "getting into serious trouble." His mother gave him three choices—one was to enter a faith-based halfway house, called Victory Outreach. He chose it and liked it, and he stayed well beyond his mother's entreaty to come home. He became a counselor there for a time. Later, because of his training at Victory Outreach, he became a counselor for the nearby City of Portland. His father's failing health and a call for help brought him to the Bay Area.

He says that when he went through the grocery store that day, "It made me realize that I've got air in my lungs, I've got spring in my legs. I can go out and find another job. Others can't. So I have it great." The young philanthropist said, "I just don't let money dictate what I do. I think that what's most important is to be able to give to your community, and you know—to see the look on some of the faces of the customers when I did it—you can't buy that feeling with all of the money in the world.

"Really, I was just trying to take a lousy day and make it a good day," Simas said, smiling broadly. "And it worked."

Meanwhile, Arthur C. Brooks' theories on generosity and increased prosperity for the giver might have some more ammunition. Just before going to press, we learned that the publicity about Michael Simas's generosity had yielded opportunities for him that he never sought in his anonymous efforts to help others that day. A film project he has worked on for years had been funded, and a job that utilizes his background in counseling had been offered, at a significant increase in salary. He couldn't believe all this had happened "just because I wanted to cheer myself up!" He said, "I guess Zig Ziglar was right: when you help others, others help you. It is just amazing."

> *Make someone happy*
> *Make just one someone happy*
> *And you will be happy too*

—Jimmy Durante

So, if circular motion brings good things back around to people who put out good things, then Jimmy Durante is right. Save a life: Make someone happy. Feed a hungry person: Make someone happy. Provide a home for the homeless: Make someone happy. And you will be happy too.

Love Is the Answer

Few readers will be old enough to remember Durante singing this famous song, but those who do remember it will recognize that the next line is, "Love is the answer ..." Interestingly, some deep thinkers agree with him on that. But a lot of us are conflicted about the word *love*.

English, you will note, has pitifully few words that mean we really care about something or someone. While the Greeks had four distinct words that accurately reflected positive feelings toward people and things, we describe our super comfortable office chair and how we feel about our new car with our word *love*. It is used to express both the slightest form of happiness and satisfaction with an item and the deepest, most meaningful communion between two souls. The word is, frankly, stretched beyond the breaking point. So to stretch the meaning even further, consider the fact that many see love as the very basis of philanthropy.

Love: The Foundation of Philanthropy

We believe that the following words of philanthropist, donor advocate, and speaker Dr. Gray Keller that describe love as the foundation of philanthropy perfectly describe the basis for real world-changing generosity.

> Love is the foundation for philanthropy. The Greek etymology is 'love' of mankind from *philos* and *anthrops*. When love is the foundation, then one of the very first acts of love is listening. Love listens to the hearts and souls of others ... When you listen carefully to both what is being said and what is not being said, you will be in a posture to learn. When learning occurs, then you will know what others truly need. You will begin to understand deeper problems than what the surface may reveal. When you learn about real needs, then you can begin to participate in a loving relationship to bring real solutions to social problems. This will allow you to get to the place of bringing real liberation to human bondage. When liberation occurs, human flourishing begins to blossom. This ultimately is the entire framework for philanthropy. A model built on love, established through listening, motivated by learning and culminating in liberating others from bondage or producing real solutions for human flourishing. And even though money, team work, systems thinking, proven strategies, leadership and participatory action

will all be needed, remember the foundation
for philanthropy is first and foremost love.

Our focus in this book will be on meeting basic human needs first, including food, water, clothing, shelter, and health. It requires us to harness our love for mankind to effect works that impact individuals on a case-by-case basis and move next to complex issues that include provision of orphanages for parentless children, educating the illiterate, training adults in job- and agriculture-related skills, and attempts to break the cycle of multigenerational poverty.

It includes supporting efforts to alleviate physical suffering plus activities that advocate for the freedom of individuals, like rescuing young boys and girls and women from sex slavery, as well as ending other forms of bondage. But world-changing generosity is not limited to taking care of physical needs. In fact, many consider giving to eliminate spiritual poverty and spiritual hunger their ultimate act of love.

What the world needs now is our energy, either in the form of direct help, like filling plates in a soup kitchen, or from the financial gift that comes from the energy you exchange for a paycheck. It's all action. It's all circular. It's all love. The more of us who get involved, the faster we can change the world.

> *What I gave, I have. What I saved and what I spent, I lost.*
>
> —Gravestone epitaph

CHAPTER THREE

THE SCORE CARD: WE'RE WINNING

It takes a noble man to plant a seed for a tree that will some day give shade to people he may never meet.

—D. ELTON TRUEBLOOD (1900–1994),
AMERICAN QUAKER AND THEOLOGIAN,
FORMER CHAPLAIN TO HARVARD AND
STANFORD UNIVERSITIES

Before he was born, Matwaru's parents took a small loan from the owner of a brick kiln in a village in India. In exchange, his parents and their children were expected to work in the kiln until they repaid the advance. But the advance was just a tool the owner used to trap them in bonded labor.

Matwaru is now forty-five years old. He began working in the brick kiln alongside his parents when he was five years old, when other children might be starting school. Matwaru never knew how much the original advance was, or the rate of interest. He just knew that, like his parents before him, he belonged to the kiln.

MATWARU AND HIS FAMILY
PHOTO COURTESY OF JUSTICE VENTURES INTERNATIONAL

Matwaru, his family, and the other slaves lived in mud huts on a plot of land designated by the kiln owner. They were given no food, so in the few hours that they were not at the kiln, they tried to find some way to feed themselves. Every morning at around 4 a.m., they walked from their huts to the kiln, where they worked until late in the night. They worked every day; there was no such thing as a day off.

If they made any mistakes, they were beaten; if they tried to escape or do some other work, the owner sent men to beat them and drag them back. They were hopeless and helpless. Matwaru said through a translator, "There was no way to save us."

Help came in late 2009, when Justice Ventures International, a US-based charity, learned of Matwaru's plight. The organization works for justice in cases similar to this all over the world, and it immediately initiated efforts with the Indian government to rescue Matwaru and forty-eight other victims who were enslaved at the kiln. Following the rescue, the organization began prosecuting the kiln owner for his crimes under Indian law and is now working to ensure that Matwaru and all those who were enslaved receive the vital government rehabilitation benefits to which released bonded laborers are entitled.

There may have been international lawyers at the forefront of this effort, but the act of saving this village of enslaved people was also made possible by the many gifts received from heroes like you—whose hearts were and are led to stop slavery everywhere it exists. Each of them opened the door to free this man, his family, and his village.

This chapter isn't for the faint of heart. It is full of statistics and facts about people who are hurting. But we hope you'll be able to see the amazing improvements that have been made because of individuals doing whatever they could do to address a critical need.

That was how Matwaru was freed. But there are lots of

other needs in the world, and this chapter will give you a quick overview of some of the most pressing worldwide issues we face, including

- hunger;
- unsafe drinking water;
- illness;
- slavery: labor, commercial sex; and
- poverty.

Hunger

Hunger kills more people every year than AIDS, malaria, and tuberculosis combined, according to the United Nations World Food Programme. Roughly 805 million people in the world do not have enough food to lead a healthy, active life. That's about one in nine people on earth. The vast majority of the world's hungry people live in developing countries, where 13.5 percent of the population is undernourished. Poor nutrition causes nearly half (45 percent) of deaths in children under five, or 3.1 million children each year.

It is encouraging that the number of chronically undernourished has fallen from an estimated 868 million between 2010 and 2012 to 842 million between 2011 and 2014, according to the United Nations. That means that *twenty million people have been taken off the hunger rolls within two years.* According to revised estimates, between 1990 and 1992, about 23.6 percent of people in developing countries were undernourished. So if current rates of progress continue, the prevalence of undernourishment in the developing world would have approached 13 percent by 2013—a 10 percent improvement. This progress is due to the support given to charitable efforts that feed the hungry and teach farming techniques that can supply food to entire villages.

HUNGRY CHILDREN IN DELHI, INDIA
PAUL PRESCOTT / SHUTTERSTOCK.COM

The number of those who are chronically undernourished has fallen from an estimated 868 million between 2010 and 2012 to 842 million between 2011 and 2014, according to the United Nations. That means that *twenty million people have been taken off the hunger rolls within two years.*

Water

But other needs are just as daunting. According to the US Centers for Disease Control and Prevention (CDC), there are more than 780 million people in the world without clean water.

780 MILLION STILL NEED CLEAN WATER
MARTCHAN / SHUTTERSTOCK.COM

Between 1990 and 2010, because of the efforts of people committed to bringing clean water to those who suffer without it, more than two billion people gained access to improved drinking water through well-digging, purification, and other clean-water efforts. But more needs to be done. The CDC reports 2,200 continue to die each day from diseases spread by dirty water supplies.

Illness Prevention

More than 20,000 children die daily from preventable illnesses. These are diseases that are regularly controlled in many parts of the world through vaccination and other common health practices that are unavailable in many regions. For example, although polio has been virtually eradicated throughout most of the world, it remains endemic in Afghanistan, Nigeria, and Pakistan.

However, great progress has been made in the reduction of deaths of children from preventable illnesses worldwide. Prior to 1990, 40,000 of the world's children used to die each day. In the 1990s, that number dropped to 33,000 per day. By 2008, it was down to 24,000, and in 2012, it was approaching 20,000. So the number of children dying before their fifth birthday has been cut in half *in less than thirty years*. Globally in the last ten years, new infections of all kinds have been reduced by 16 percent. But there is so much more to be done.

> Prior to 1990, 40,000 of the world's children used to die each day. In the 1990s, that number dropped to 33,000 per day. By 2008, it was down to 24,000, and in 2012, it was approaching 20,000. So the number of children dying before their fifth birthday has been cut in half *in less than thirty years*.

Measles

Worldwide, measles is a killer. At its peak, measles was killing 1.5 million people every year. In the last eight years, the number of children dying from measles has declined 78 percent, from more than 700,000 each year to fewer than 165,000.

Malaria

Although five hundred million people will contract malaria this year, the malaria rate in twenty-two countries has been cut in half in a period of six years, and malaria infections have decreased by nineteen million per year. Between 2005 and 2009, malaria deaths dropped by 140,000 per year. Between 2000 and 2012, the global mortality rate was reduced by 45 percent because of efforts supported by innumerable donors. Can we reduce that again by half? Clearly, with enough support we can.

Small Pox

Meanwhile, small pox, once a vicious killer on the loose, has been eradicated.

HIV/AIDS

At one time, any child born of a mother suffering from HIV/AIDS was sure to contract the disease and die of it. One effort that began in 1971 to provide medical care to victims of war and disaster has addressed this issue. It reported that by 2007 it had safely delivered more than 100,000 babies and treated more than 100,000 HIV/AIDS patients.

Repair of Cleft Lips and Palates

A charity started in 1982 to treat children born with facial deformities performed reconstructive surgeries on more than 120,000 patients by 2008.

Slavery: Labor, Commercial Sex

It may be hard to believe, but there are more people in the world in slavery today than at any time in history. Almost twenty-one million men, women, and children are held in some type of forced labor, according to a 2014 report by the General Labor Office in Geneva, Switzerland. Human trafficking does not mean that people are necessarily moved from one place to another; it is a term that indicates commercial use. Trafficking in commercial sex is the fastest-growing and second-largest criminal industry in the world, generating $32 billion a year. Between 600,000 and 800,000 people are trafficked internationally every year.

> Major organizations involved in fighting human trafficking estimate that between 20.9 million and 27 million men, women, and children are held in some type of bondage.

Half of all modern-day slaves are children who were either abducted or sold into slavery by their parents or guardians. Nearly 75 percent are female. It is estimated by the Congressional Research Service that as many as 700,000 young girls and women are abducted every year in the worldwide human trafficking network, in which girls as young as twelve are being forced to become sex slaves. It is shocking for many in the US to learn that between 100,000 and 300,000 American children become victims every year.

NEARLY 75 PERCENT OF MODERN-DAY SLAVES ARE FEMALE.

Shared Hope International is committed to bringing justice to victims of sex trafficking by supporting the development of policies and legislation on the state, federal, and global levels against those who create the demand for underage sex services. The organization issues a report card every year. States that received an overall grade of F in 2013 are California, Hawaii, Maine, Michigan, Pennsylvania, and South Dakota. These states had the lowest records of prosecuting and punishing the buyers of child sex services and the least protective laws for victims of child sex trafficking and abuse.

In spite of the fact that we hear the bad news about the endless need throughout the world, there is also news of victory.

Because of the increased involvement and support of freedom and justice organizations, restitution has been made to many victims of sex trafficking, forced labor, wrongful imprisonment, religious persecution, and other injustices.

In one recent twelve-week period in North India, seventy-two victims of sex trafficking were set free, including sixteen minors who were found in a Delhi brothel. The rescue was a joint effort by a single US-based charity (Justice Ventures International), local police, and several Delhi-based nongovernment organization (NGO) partners.

A total of thirteen traffickers were arrested in the Delhi case, and the girls were connected with rehabilitation services. Justice Ventures' lawyers continue to work toward the prosecution of the traffickers for their crimes. Their work to free enslaved people and the work of many other such organizations continues unabated to this day with the help of funds supplied by supporters.

Poverty

Poverty is the root from which grows deprivation of all kinds. Hunger, homelessness, lack of health care, lack of immunization, child mortality, illiteracy, and child labor are some of the major offshoots. Educational efforts, the provision of basic necessities like electricity, and the development of rudimentary economies are being employed in small measure to fight poverty and change lives.

It is surprising, for many of us, that more than half of the world lives on less than $2.50 a day. In contrast, the average American teenager spends nearly $85 every week, according to Teenage Research Unlimited; the average American earns $105 per day or $38,611 per year.

INDIA HAS THE LARGEST NUMBER OF PEOPLE
LIVING BELOW THE INTERNATIONAL POVERTY LINE.
JAN S. / SHUTTERSTOCK.COM

At the same time, there are 1.6 billion people in the world with no electricity, a luxury that we take for granted until a storm inconveniences us by temporarily cutting off our access. Telephones, computers, heating devises, and water pumps all work on electricity, so none are available in these regions.

Dire poverty forces one in seven children worldwide (158 million) to go to work every day. Nearly every second child, 1 billion out of the 2.2 billion children in the world, lives in poverty.

Illiteracy may be the chain that permanently ties the poor to their limited existences. Almost one billion people in the world can't read or write their own name. Nearly 100 million children throughout the world are denied a basic education.

Homelessness for the poor is almost a given. More than one billion people in the world lack what we would consider to be adequate shelter, and about 100 million of them have no housing whatsoever. Roughly 30 million of those live in the world's urban centers.

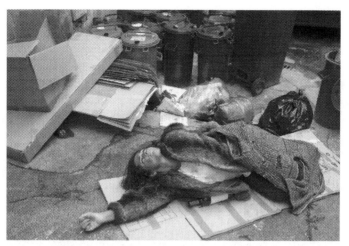

THE US HAS THE LARGEST NUMBER OF HOMELESS
WOMEN AMONG INDUSTRIALIZED NATIONS.

In the US, it is estimated that there could be as many as 3.5 million homeless (1 percent of our population), including 1.5 million children. These kids are twice as likely to experience hunger and far more likely to have chronic health issues. Their estimated high school graduation rate is only 22 percent.

> In the US there could be as many as 3.5 million homeless (1 percent of our population), including 1.5 million children. These kids are twice as likely to experience hunger and far more likely to have chronic health issues. Their estimated high school graduation rate is only 22 percent.

In excess of one in seven Americans is now receiving benefits from the Supplemental Nutrition Assistance Program, which means that more than 47 million of our own citizens, 15 percent of our nation's population, is on food stamps. That's more than twenty-two million households, which impacts one in every five of our children.

The statistics are alarming. But much is being done. Improvement in every area of need has been made over the past two or three decades by individuals who learned of an issue that struck a chord in their hearts and, like the young man, began throwing starfish into the ocean. You can't save everyone, but together we can save a few, and those few add up quickly.

Literacy rates are climbing rapidly. Because access to books is the number-one deterrent to reading deficiencies, a charity formed to fight illiteracy distributed 16.6 million books to 4.6 million children between 1966 and 2007.

Meanwhile, Habitat for Humanity, established in 1976, mobilized volunteers on behalf of the homeless to build 800,000 homes by 2013.

In 1981, more than half of the world's population lived in extreme poverty. In 2005, that number was down to 25 percent—poverty was cut in half in just one generation. The new focus is getting the remaining 1.1 billion people living in extreme poverty—on less than $1.25 per day—out of poverty by 2030.

No Accident

We hope you will get excited and be encouraged by the progress that has been made, because every good thing was accomplished by a deliberate and focused assault by lots of people on a particular evil. This is a war we are winning—and will win, with your help.

None of these positive trends have been accidents. Every single person who was sick, poverty stricken, starving, in slavery, or without clean water was helped by the charitable efforts of everyday folks who decided to care enough to do what they could do.

These positive results are a direct result of personal generosity, the kind that changes the world, one starfish at a time. The kind that is produced by regular people, rich and poor, who love, care, give, play, lead happy lives, who are evolved and love sunshine, baseball, and hotdogs ... people like all of us.

CHAPTER FOUR

A PARADIGM SHIFT: MOVING FROM SELFISH TO SELFLESS

*Money, pardon the expression, is like manure.
It's not worth a thing unless it's spread around,
encouraging young things to grow.*

—DOLLY LEVI, *HELLO, DOLLY!*

Aidan Hornaday was just another bored seven-year-old kid as he rummaged through his older brother's things, looking for some kind of diversion.

AIDAN HORNADAY
PHOTO BY STAN KAADY

At the bottom of a box was his brother's dusty harmonica. With no idea how to play it, Aidan looked for a button to turn it on. By the next night he was sounding pretty good. As he waited for his mom at a restaurant in Vinings, Georgia, just across the Chattahoochee River from Atlanta, he took off his hat and began to play. People in the restaurant liked what they heard and began putting tips in his hat. Aidan made $80 in one night. He couldn't believe it. What would he do with all that money?

Aidan had recently heard about African orphans who, with no clean water, were battling—and often dying of—intestinal parasites. He had read that medications to treat the disease were available. Four pills cost a dollar and would be administered by a charity working in the area. For $80, he could buy 320 pills! Which he did. Aidan's problem: solved.

People heard about Aidan, and he began playing for and speaking to others—quite a few others. By the time Aidan was thirteen years old, a little more than five years later, he had raised and donated more than $90,000 from playing his harmonica and sharing his heart, allowing others to give from their passion. He has performed for audiences of one to audiences of thousands, often sharing the stage with top musicians.

Through his desire to serve and make a difference, Aidan met a young man named Brayden Martin who had been diagnosed with brain and spinal cancer at age two and had endured five years of nonstop treatment. Brayden used a wheelchair, was on multiple medications, and had been through unrelenting rounds of chemotherapies, requiring constant medical visits far from his home.

Brayden's mom had challenges of her own. With another child to care for and no car, getting him in his wheelchair back and forth to medical visits was tremendously difficult and often impossible.

Aidan bonded with this boy over music, playing games and being a friend, often helping during hospital stays. Yet he wanted to do more. After months of trying, Aidan convinced a local car dealer to donate an SUV to the family, which, incidentally, has a place for a wheelchair in the back.

"It's one of the greatest, most rewarding things ever," he says. "You get more [from life] when you help. Blessings just come—it's amazing." His purpose now is to teach all generations the necessity and joy of giving.

Who Do You Think You Are?

So much of our happiness is based upon what we think about ourselves. Aidan is not a child of great wealth. There are no limousines in his life. He doesn't have an entourage. What makes him powerful is that he doesn't believe there are *haves* and *have-nots*. Nor does he believe that one can never have enough money or that a person must be rich to enjoy spreading some money and effort around on behalf of others.

Believe it or not, if you're a member of middle-class America, you are one of the haves. The haves, like Aidan, have everything they need, because they know it to be true. The haves who think they are have-nots will never have enough because they believe *that* to be true. Aidan thinks and acts like a powerful person because he is. Change the way you think, and you change the way you act.

Although Americans maintain the top earning levels in the world, individuals in the US give an average of only 2 percent of what they earn to help others. And that average includes giving by American billionaires, which means that a huge percentage of Americans give nothing. Why is this so?

It could be for want of a map. We all have a map we use to navigate our lives. We give or do not give because our parents did or did not. We may drive the way our father did or belong to the same club our mother belonged to. These maps can be helpful diagrams for our lives or they can be crippling markers that leave us with the tendencies toward addictive practices or worse.

> The haves like Aidan have everything they need because they know it to be true. The haves who think they are have-nots will never have enough because they know *that* to be true. Aidan thinks and acts like a powerful person, because he is. Change the way you think and you change the way you act.

A favorite family saying might have been "generosity begins at home," the by-word of a generation that lived through the Depression and stopped any trickle of giving that might have gone on before—and might now do them a world of good. Interestingly, at the same time, the Great Depression caused many with very little to share in the generosity movement.

Many a beggar saw the telling marks on the curb in front of those homes where the lady of the house would let you sit on the back porch and feed you a meal, maybe give you some paying work to do as you passed through town. Nancy's grandmother was a woman with two children and a husband in long-term hospital care. She was one of the angels of mercy to the hungry during those dark days. She didn't count the cost, just shared whatever she had.

Others are collectors of money. Often, their great joy of the people who can afford to give the most is to watch the numbers in their bank account or portfolio creep higher and the zeros multiply with every paycheck or wise investment. Many times, their goal is to leave large sums to the kids. They feel, somehow, that their self-worth is tied up in all those zeros.

The fact is that money is nothing more than an exchange rate for your energy. The person with too much debt is having his or her energy usurped by interest payments; the interest collector is letting his energy sit on a shelf, unused, when there are so many who desperately need help.

A Paradigm Shift

The groundbreaking research conducted by Jordan Grafman, PhD, showed us in Chapter Two that our brains are actually wired to be generous. But against our deepest instincts to glue our dollar bills into our pockets or go broke paying for the latest state-of-the-art consumer goods, we can turn the current paradigm upside down.

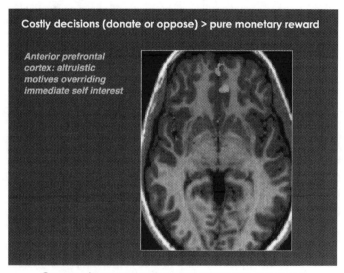

Costly decisions (donate or oppose) > pure monetary reward

Anterior prefrontal cortex: altruistic motives overriding immediate self interest

GRAFMAN'S BRAIN STUDIES ILLUMINATE THE FACT THAT
DECIDING TO GIVE IS BETTER THAN TO RECEIVE.

Imagine, instead of Americans being primarily self-interested, we decide to become inherently selfless.

Instead of most of us aspiring to buy the next material thing we are convinced we need to make ourselves happy, the majority of people now understand that the feeling they get when they help another far outweighs a new purchase or even bigger number in their investment portfolio. Instead they invest in others, helping them to live better lives.

What if instead of thinking only about what we can get, Americans dreamed about what we can give? What if when somebody gives us something, our thoughts immediately turn to how we can pay it forward to help somebody else? Imagine that this process has become so commonplace that, instead of assuming that others are scheming about what they can get out of us, we count on them to be generous.

> Instead of most of us aspiring to buy the next material thing that we are convinced we need to make ourselves happy, the majority of people now understand that the feeling they get when they help another far outweighs a new purchase or even bigger number in their investment portfolio.

A Sense of Community

When the focus is off ourselves and onto others, a feeling of isolation is replaced with a strong sense of community with other generous people wherever we go. We understand that there is plenty for ourselves even as we share with others. The death grip on our possessions has loosened, and each has the freedom to give what they can and want to share.

Now, as never before, givers have the opportunity to spot needs and feed into them as they feel they should. As a group, givers are now vastly more powerful, because everyone gives who has the capacity to give—a lot or a little. By doing so, they change the world in an earthshaking way. All this is a result of changing the way we look at the world. And these people are making a colossal difference.

The Times They Are a-Changin'

Here's an encouraging indication that such a culture of generosity is taking hold. In 2012, a coalition of more than 1,400 charities teamed up to provide a break from overexposure to commercialization during the start of the Christmas shopping season; they launched Giving Tuesday, a day on which we were encouraged to shift our focus from shopping to charitable giving. In 2013, following the shopping sprees of Gray Thursday, Black Friday, Small Business Saturday, and Cyber Monday, 8,300 charities benefitted from Giving Tuesday.

We are coming to understand that to love means to be generous, and to be generous means to give our time, effort, and financial resources to others. Don't be scared by the idea of giving. Nobody expects you to begin eating Ramen noodles full time (as delicious as they are). It just means we give something rather than keep it ourselves. We are giving up whatever that dollar would have bought so that someone else can have what they need.

Giving until it hurts to give? Well, that's another level, but you've got to start somewhere. Your start might look like this: you have decided that an hour of your time to coach a team of neighborhood kids is an hour you can afford to give to some children who need a leader in their lives. You have figured out that you can give up some tired TV shows on Friday night to help serve food and counsel men at a homeless shelter. Or maybe you've made room in your budget to fund a hunger program in Africa or across town. How long can we make this list? It can go on as long as the imaginations of every reader we have.

Experts suggest that those who never give to charitable causes, which the National Center for Charitable Statistics says amounted to 33 percent of the US in 2006, start with small giving. Like learning to ski, a person has to start on the bunny hill to get some practice and taste a little of the thrill that the experienced skiers and givers feel. That way they will learn by doing and can help some people who need it as they figure out their side of the equation.

Some small giving opportunities are so much fun that they inspire a group mentality that, through social media, creates a virus of small good deeds that grow to produce a large result.

The Ice Bucket Challenge

In the late summer of 2014 a phenomenon called the Ice Bucket Challenge swept the nation, giving a lot of people an opportunity to experience the benefits of their own paradigm shift in consciousness. This kind of philanthropy is—seriously—so much fun and so crazy that it appeals to the child in adults everywhere. And perhaps because of that, it raised lots of money from generous people.

It works like this. A person shoots a video of himself dumping a bucket of ice water over his head and issues a challenge to friends who are named in the video. They have to either dump a bucket of ice water over their own heads within forty-eight hours or send $100 to the ALS charity of their choice.

ALS, short for Amyotrophic Lateral Sclerosis, is better known as Lou Gehrig's disease. It is an illness of a thousand days, attacking bodily functions while leaving the brain intact, so that victims are witness to the ravenous decline of their bodies. It is a disease without treatment or cure.

It all started when an ice bucket challenge (tied to no particular charity) was issued to a golfer by the name of Chris Kennedy, who designated his contribution to go to ALS because he had a family member suffering from the disease. Kennedy posted the video on Facebook July 15, 2014, publicly challenging his cousin, Jeanette Senerchia, whose husband Anthony had ALS. She took the challenge and posted her video with the hashtag #StrikeOutALS.

The small town where the family lives caught on to the challenge, which spread like wildfire, reaching other ALS patients, their families, their friends and hometowns. By that time, the Ice Bucket Challenge belonged to ALS; the ALS Association started seeing an unexplained and dramatic rise in donations. By the end of August, more than $100 million had been raised, and awareness of ALS had hit an all-time high.

Kennedy said that his goal had just been to "put a smile on Anthony's face and bring some awareness to this terrible disease." But as fate would have it, he and others, like Pat Quinn and Pete Frates, had ignited a national effort to equip the ALS Association with the research money it needs to fight the killing fields of ALS. And every Ice Bucket Challenge check-writer stands on the front lines with the researchers in this fight. Hundreds of them, even thousands of them, will attest to the best cold-water shower of their lives.

The Ice Bucket Challenge and other efforts of this type are a great way to get your generous feet wet (literally in this case), giving those who are beginning to view themselves differently the opportunity to experience the benefits of the shift from self-interest to selflessness.

Crowdfunding

Another way to get your feet wet (in this case without literally getting them wet) is participating in a fairly new giving mechanism. Many opportunities to contribute to causes that appeal to your personal beliefs and passions are now available to you online through crowdsourcing platforms. Crowdfunding is web-based collaboration of a large number of people who collectively provide needed funding through relatively small individual contributions.

There are two types of crowdsourcing platforms that support charity: donation-based, in which no compensation is expected, and reward-based, in which an incentive is provided through nonfinancial rewards, like a token or a first-edition release of a product. The other two platforms are not charity related. They support business start-ups, as well as growth, by raising equity funding and providing business loans.

The Crowdfunding Industry Report for 2012 said that the number of crowdfunding websites had increased from about one hundred in 2007 to 452 by April 2012; the report estimated that the number would reach 536 by the end of that year. More than

$1.5 billion was raised through one million successful campaigns on crowdsourcing platforms, and the report predicted that total funds raised through this method would nearly double in 2012.

The Shift That Shapes

Making the shift in one's thinking is more than an exercise in shaping a more generous you. The change in outlook can affect your body as well as your mind.

People use the phrase "doing well by doing good" when they are talking about people or companies that make money in a business that benefits others. But you don't have to be a corporation to benefit from a generous life. Individuals can do well by doing good too.

Check out these facts:

- A Cornell University study showed that volunteering increases a person's energy.
- University of Michigan research, conducted over a ten-year period with 2,700 people, concluded that death rates of men who volunteered were two and a half times lower over those ten years than those who did not volunteer.
- Harvard University researchers found that giving is such a powerful immune booster that the effect can be experienced just by witnessing the act.

Generosity also makes us more active and involved, impacting our work in positive ways. In 2012, researchers from the University of Pennsylvania and the University of Michigan split fundraisers into two groups. One group was asked to record journal entries about contributions they had made to help others, and the second group wrote about memories of receiving something. Researchers measured how many fundraising calls each group made two weeks before and two weeks after recording these experiences. The fundraisers who wrote about *giving* made 29 percent more calls in the second two weeks, but those who wrote about receiving showed no change in activity.

The second experiment involved three groups of college students. They were told to write down either three ways they had received help or three foods they had recently eaten. When the students returned three weeks later to pick up their payment for participating, they were given a form describing the 2011 tsunami in Japan. They were asked if they would like to contribute a portion of their payment to the tsunami fund. More than 25 percent donated to the cause; those who had reflected on the generosity of others were more than twice as likely to donate.

As givers, it is clear that the more directly we experience the impact that our giving has on another, the more we benefit. Giving has also been widely shown to be an antidote to self-criticism and depression. It's pretty simple: the more we focus on others, the healthier we are and the more productive we are.

You might think such a change is your gift to others, when in fact it is a gift to yourself and to your family. Generosity, the antidote to consumerism and self-involvement, is a joy-giving, contentment-yielding exercise in passion for mankind—the medicine to fight sadness. Changing the world for others also changes the world for you.

Ultimately, when a critical mass of people make a paradigm shift from self-interest to selflessness, only one result is possible: The world will be changed to a more peaceful, in sync, healthier, productive, and loving planet on which to live.

CHAPTER FIVE

SPENDING AND GIVING: LIVING AND GIVING TO THE FULLEST

Make your money your god and it will plague you like the devil.

—HENRY FIELDING (1707–1754), ENGLISH NOVELIST

Goldfish crackers or money. It's all the same.

If someone handed you $100, what would you do with it? That was the challenge for forty-four college students participating in the Mercy Works Synergy program in Syracuse in 2012. Those kids weren't rich. In fact, some were just getting by, but although they might have been tempted to buy new clothes, a video game, or a nice meal, the assignment was to give the money away. Further, they had only days to do it and prepare a report about the experience.

One student had been homeless the year before, so she decided to give her $100 to Salvation Army's Barnabas House where she had stayed. She wanted to "give back to other teens."

Another sent money to his seventeen-year-old cousin who was in jail, and another bought baby supplies for a pregnant younger sister. One young woman bought bed linens and decorations for an eighteen-year-old transient who finally had a room of her own.

"Her shock just made my day," said the young woman. "How she reacted to having received these small items I take for granted really opened my eyes."

The students learned important lessons about charity, kindness, and generosity—exactly the reaction organizers had in mind when funding the money giveaway. Said Bill Reichardt, one of the organizers, "Long ago we realized the power of giving and the joy it brings." He and other donors wanted to bring some of that joy to these college students so that they would enter the world as adults knowing the power of generosity.

Through the Mercy Works Synergy program, students found out that people actually find more happiness in spending money on others than spending it on themselves. This finding is reinforced by a lot of interesting research. But the research that was most entertaining involved toddlers and goldfish crackers.

In individual trials, toddlers were given goldfish crackers. To the last child, they found that children were happiest when sharing the crackers with the investigator's monkey puppet instead of gobbling them all themselves. Hmm.

So maybe that axiom "money can't buy happiness" is wrong. Money *can* buy happiness. You just have to spend it right ... or share it right.

What Can You Do?

You can spend your money to accumulate more and more stuff, or you can give what you can, along with others who are determined to change the world.

Where Does The Money Go?

The US holds the trophy for being the richest nation on earth, so it would follow that even the way we dispose of trash costs a bundle. In fact according to a 2003 article in *Fast Company*, Americans spent more annually on trash bags than nearly half of the world did on all goods consumed.

We live in a culture of consumerism.

How can we help it? We're bombarded with advertising messages. The average American is exposed to thousands of ads a day. Print or electronic versions of morning newspapers and television news all hit us with ads at home before we leave for work. Then we listen to the radio and see billboards as we drive; we encounter magazines in the doctor's waiting room, ads on our smart phones, and pop-ups when we're working on our computers.

We're constantly being told that we are incomplete in some way without the product or service being promoted. "Buy this. Buy that. You'll look better. You'll smell better. You'll look younger. You'll live longer."

Although Americans are pretty big spenders all year long, we bring out the really big purchasing guns at Christmas. Black Friday, which begins at midnight on Thanksgiving, has been joined by Gray Thursday, for those who can't even wait until midnight.

Since 2010, the following day has come to be recognized as Small Business Saturday, a day on which shoppers are encouraged to buy from small local stores. And two days later, on Cyber Monday, savvy marketers have convinced a good portion of our country to shop online, now accounting for more than $2 billion in sales.

In 2013, retail sales over this long weekend totaled $57.4 billion, according to the *Christian Science Monitor*. Total retail sales for the Christmas season have been reported to be as high as $450 billion. That's an average of $1,400 per person.

In the same fourth quarter of 2013, US households took on $241 billion in additional debt. Whether it is because of a bigger house, a newer car, or a mountain of consumer goods, unmanageable debt can take away one of our most meaningful opportunities: the freedom to give.

The Debt Debacle

While our nation is struggling under what seems like insurmountable debt of more than $18 trillion at the end of 2014, American households feel the pinch even more, because unlike the federal government, they can't print money.

Even if you are paying off college loans, credit card debt, and more, you should consider giving something. Maybe just your time. Maybe a donation of things you no longer need. Make an effort to provide something for others. It works.

In fact, it is great if there's a way to give actual money as debt is paid off. There is plenty of anecdotal evidence from folks who believe they broke free of debt even more quickly because they never stopped giving. In any case, there are organizations that can help get rid of debt and restore financial piece of mind. Check the WorldChangingGenerosity.com website, under the Resources tab, for links.

> While our nation is struggling under what seems like insurmountable debt of more than $18 trillion at the end of 2014, American households overall are in even more trouble, because, unlike the federal government, households can't print money.

Are Americans addicted to consumerism? From *Money Questions That Matter* come these facts:

- The average American shops six hours a week and spends only forty minutes playing with his or her children.
- It is estimated that Americans focus on 250 ads per day.
- By age twenty, we've seen one million commercials.
- More Americans declare bankruptcy than graduate college.
- Money is a factor in 90 percent of divorces.
- According to mental health professionals,
  - purchasing pleasure disappears quickly;
  - the more you have, the less you're satisfied;
  - the more you have, the more you have to worry about;
  - the more you have, the more you have to lose; and
  - the more you have, the more you want.

Never Enough

It seems that enough is never enough. In 1950, each American consumed an average of 144 pounds of meat and poultry per year. By 2007, that number increased 54 percent to 222 pounds per person. In 1950, there was one car for every fifty people in the United States, a total of about 53 million cars. Today, that number has skyrocketed 467 percent to about 300 million.

We live in an era with television programs called *Hoarders, Storage Wars,* and *Auction Hunters,* which all highlight an epidemic that is permeating our society: the unhealthy obsession with accumulating as much stuff as possible. Watch any of these shows and it becomes painfully clear that the more people accumulate, the less happy they become—certainly less generous. And if the psychiatrists are right, they are more worried and fearful to boot.

In their book *The Paradox of Generosity, Giving We Receive, Grasping We Lose,* coauthors Christian Smith, PhD, and Hilary Davidson share research that clearly illustrates that the more people practice giving of their time, talent, and economic resources, the happier and healthier they are. Conversely, by holding on to what we have, we lose out on what we might have gained.

Their research showed that those who gave away 10 percent or more of their income were much happier than those who gave away less than 10 percent. But fewer than 3 percent of Americans give at that level.

Although it's clear that being self-focused with your resources can be detrimental to your health and happiness, research from the Science of Generosity Initiatives (University of Notre Dame) reports that 86 percent of Americans give away 2 percent or less of their incomes, and almost 45 percent give away nothing.

We are programmed to believe that buying things will bring happiness, but clearly that's not working. According to the CDC, more than thirty-one million people in the US suffer from the symptoms of depression, about twice as many as in Russia, where goods are far less available. The truth is all the junk in the world—even if it is good junk—will not make you happy over time. What we all should all be asking is, how can we use our money (energy) to be happy and impact the world in a positive way?

> We live in an era with television programs called called *Hoarders, Storage Wars,* and *Auction Hunters,* which all highlight an epidemic that is permeating our society: the sick obsession with accumulating as much *stuff* as possible.

Happy Money

Interestingly, a pair of renowned researchers has been working to find answers to that very question. According to *Happy Money: The Science of Smarter Spending,* written by behavioral scientists Dr. Elizabeth Dunn and Dr. Michael Norton, there are four questions people should ask themselves about their spending intentions:

1. Does this bring me together with other people?
2. Will this make a memorable story that I will tell for years to come?
3. Is this experience in line with who I am or who I'd like to become?
4. Is this a unique opportunity and something I can't compare to things I've done before?

Think of the possibilities! You could go to India with a group to build houses for Untouchables or serve dinner to the poor on a regular basis at a local shelter; teach someone to read or help a cleanup effort in a neighboring state after a tornado; donate to free children from the sex trade or counsel troubled teens. Does none of that sound like you? Make your own list. Helping others is a sure way to check off all four of the Dunn and Norton principles.

The doctors go a step further. Of the five issues that keep

people from enjoying their money, this one stands out: "You're investing too much in yourself and not enough in other people."

Naturally, we think that the happier we are with ourselves, the more likely it is that we'll bring happiness to others. But Dunn and Norton have found that the opposite is true. If you make others happier first, you'll bring yourself happiness in the process. This might be an obvious fact to those who regularly invest in other's lives, but if you're new to all this, the overwhelming evidence is that it works. And the word *happiness* is just a very thin veneer over the feelings of camaraderie, success, gratefulness, and deep spiritual fulfillment you'll experience when you get together with others to solve a problem and benefit people who are not able to help themselves.

> The doctors go a step further. Of the five issues that keep people from enjoying their money, this one stands out: "You're investing too much in yourself and not enough in other people."

Dunn and Norton point out in their book that a study of more than six hundred Americans revealed that while personal spending accounts for the lion's share of most people's budgets, "the amount of money individuals devoted to themselves was unrelated to their overall happiness. What did predict happiness? The amount of money they gave away. The more they invested in others, the happier they were."

If the good doctors are right, you might wonder why donating a bag of clothing to the church rummage sale or sending money to the tsunami relief fund feels good but doesn't send you over the moon. That's because the uber-happiness kick comes from seeing and experiencing your money at work.

That means getting involved, or at least visiting the place you send your money, which—although ideal—isn't always possible. But there are a growing number of organizations that provide information on the impact of dollars donated. This is especially helpful if you are shepherding children into the practice of generous living, as kids need more feedback to understand the good they are doing to truly benefit from the experience.

> A study of more than six hundred Americans revealed that while personal spending accounts for the lion's share of most people's budgets, "the amount of money individuals devoted to themselves was unrelated to their overall happiness. What did predict happiness? The amount of money they gave away.

Charitable organizations that allow donors to see where their money goes in real time via computer are growing in numbers, and they can help a donor see their money at work—even in charities on the other side of the world.

Political Threats

It is important to remember that the individual still controls the power to change the world. Giving USA 2014, The Annual Report of Philanthropy for the Year 2013, researched and written by the Lilly Family School of Philanthropy at Indiana University, reports that individuals accounted for 72 percent of all US charitable giving: $240.6 billion out of the total of $335.17 billion.

Of greatest concern now is a move to reduce the charitable tax deduction. It is a proposal that would likely cut donations by billions of dollars—a move that would punish those at the very bottom rung of the economy of the nation and the world.

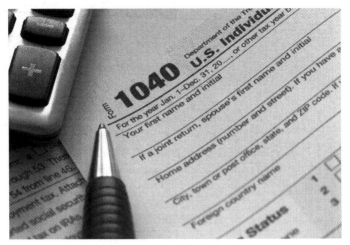

PROPOSED CUTS IN CHARITABLE DEDUCTIONS
WOULD RESTRICT GIVING.

Recent schemes would cap the charitable deduction at 28 percent, at a time when the top income tax rate on the highest earners has increased from 35 to 39.6 percent. This would raise the cost of giving to charity from 60 cents per dollar to 72 cents per dollar—a 20-percent increase in what some refer to as the charity tax. The *Chronicle of Philanthropy* reports that the reduction in giving that could result from such a cap might be as high as $9 billion a year.

> Of greatest concern now is a move to reduce a tax deduction that is predicted to cut charitable donations by billions of dollars—a move that would punish those at the very bottom rung of the nation's and the world's economy.

This amount equates to more than *the entire budgets of the American Cancer Society, Boys and Girls Clubs, Catholic Charities, Goodwill, Habitat for Humanity, Red Cross, and YMCA, combined,* and that was before the top tax rate was raised to its current level. Now that the top income tax rate has been increased, the impact of this proposal would be far more detrimental.

Volunteerism is not as strong in recent years either. According to the Bureau of Labor Statistics, in 2013 the percentage of the population volunteering was down more than 2 percent over the past decade, to 25.4 percent. Many believe the drop is due to the recession, as more and more people work longer hours to make ends meet.

So with numbers headed in the wrong direction, how can we suggest that the world-changing generosity movement can really do what we say it can do—really change the world?

How Americans Could Change the World

America has the resources to eliminate the major needs of hurting people throughout the world.

Consider:

- six billion people in the world
- three hundred million people in the United States
- the United States contains up to 5 percent of the world's population
- Americans hold 20 percent of the world's wealth

If you think that you don't have the resources necessary to take part in the World-Changing Generosity movement, visit GlobalRichList.com, select "Income," then " USA (Dollar)," input your annual net income (after tax) and see where you stand compared to the rest of the world. What you will learn is, if your annual take-home pay is $32,400 or more, you're among the top 1 percent of the richest people in the world. The average American earns $38,611 per year. A person with an annual income of $25,000 is wealthier than 90 percent of the world's population. Even our poor are rich by world standards. The poverty level for a family of four in the US is $63 a day. In richer parts of the emerging world, it is $4 a day.

Many will offer the fact that it costs more to live in the US than it does in many other places on earth, and that of course is true. But the investment involved in being a world changer is much less than you might think. As you will see, if we—who have never missed a meal—would give just a little, life could improve for most of the people on earth.

Here's the Math

According to celebrated economist Jeffrey Sachs, whose book *The End of Poverty* demonstrates his plan to eliminate extreme poverty around the world by 2025, we are standing in an advantageous window of time. The number of extremely poor people has dropped (1.1 billion from 1.5 billion in 1980) to a level that, if given enough of a boost now, we could eradicate extreme poverty, with its attendant issues of hunger, homelessness, water purity issues, and basic health care, for a cost of $124 billion dollars, based on World Bank findings.

His focus is on the one billion poorest individuals around the world who are caught in a poverty trap of disease, physical isolation, environmental stress, political instability, and lack of access to capital, technology, medicine, and education. The goal is to help these people reach the first rung on the ladder of economic development so they can rise above mere subsistence level and achieve some control over their economic futures and their lives.

If everyone in the high-income world gave 70 cents out of every $100, or seven-tenths of 1 percent, the number would be achieved. That amount would be $350 per year if you make $50,000, and $700 if you make $100,000. Not to put too fine a point on it, but that is $13.46 a week ... to

change the world.

Most would say that qualifies as a "door buster" price for world change.

The *Wall Street Journal* reported that, according to the Federal Reserve, the net worth of US households hit a record high in 2013 of $80.7 trillion—an astounding $10 trillion increase in twelve months. The rise in the value of stocks and mutual funds accounted for $5.6 trillion of that figure, and another $2.3 trillion was attributed to increase in the value of residential real estate.

> This effort should involve not just Americans but every high-income person in every first-world country where the citizens are human and blood pumped by a heart runs through their veins.

Over the next fifty years, it is predicted that between $41 trillion and $136 trillion will pass from older Americans to younger generations, suggesting that roughly $1 trillion to $3 trillion in wealth will change hands every year.

As our older generations pass away and we face the future in a world of our own making, will we spend our money to pay for the debts run up in days past? Or will we put something aside to make the world a better place?

This effort should involve not just Americans but every high-income person in every first-world country where the citizens are human and blood pumped by a heart runs through their veins.

It is now up to us. We can take part in one of the most rewarding and peaceable efforts the world has ever known, quietly, daringly giving what we can, what we consider to be right. Then, standing together, a worldwide army of givers will succeed in changing the world.

PART II: STEPPING UP

Love cannot remain by itself—it has no meaning.

Love has to be put into action and that action is service.

Whatever form we are, able or disabled, rich or poor, it is not how much we do but how much love we put into the doing; a lifelong sharing of love with others.

—MOTHER TERESA (1910–1997), ALBANIAN-BORN
INDIAN ROMAN CATHOLIC NUN WHO FOUNDED
MISSIONARIES OF CHARITY

CHAPTER SIX

SPREAD THE MOVEMENT: BE A CATALYST, TELL YOUR STORY, PAY IT FORWARD

Never doubt that a small group of thoughtful, committed citizens can change the world; indeed, it's the only thing that ever has.

—MARGARET MEAD, WORLD FAMOUS ANTHROPOLOGIST, 1901–1978

Once a Wall Street golden boy, Bill Williams felt helpless as he watched his once highly successful career as a stockbroker fall apart due to his chronic alcoholism. That wasn't all. After twenty years of drinking, he was told that his serious health issues were irreversible. At the young age of thirty-nine he heard the words, "If you don't quit now, you have, at most, six months to live."

No matter what doctors and other experts told him to try, it became clear that there was no cure for alcoholism.

Then, in December 1934, Williams found himself being treated again at New York City's Towns Hospital. But this time while in their care, he underwent what he later described as a spiritual transformation.

As a result of the application of principles from a nondenominational religious movement called the Oxford Group, Williams was able to begin living without alcohol. He began practicing a formula that involved performing a self-inventory, admitting mistakes, righting wrongs, praying, meditating, and carrying the message to others.

Williams was sober and at peace for the first time in many, many years.

Then on a business trip to Akron, Ohio, in 1935, Williams

met Dr. Bob Smith, a successful physician who had fought alcoholism all of his adult life with no success. They shared their struggles. With William's help and the program he had followed, "Dr. Bob" emerged from under the influence of addiction as well. The two then developed the Twelve Step program using many of the Oxford Group's methods and began using the steps in small groups, helping others to sobriety.

To promote the program, Wilson and others wrote the book, *Alcoholics Anonymous: The Story of How More Than One Hundred Men Have Recovered from Alcoholism*, from which AA drew its name.

Then, once the AA program was established, Bill W. and Dr. Bob got out of the way. That's right. Rather than trying to build an AA empire by controlling the expansion or using the program to make money, they just let go. Nobody owns AA. Wilson called it a "benign anarchy." Another AA leader says the organization "looks like it couldn't survive, as there's no leadership or top-level executive telling locals what to do."

Equipped with only the Twelve Steps and the sponsor concept (a fellow alcoholic, who has been through the program, holds another accountable), chapters have been established throughout the world. Nobody really knows how many thousands of chapters exist today or how many millions of people have been helped, but the point is that the numbers don't matter, because this decentralized movement works for alcoholics—individual alcoholics, who don't care if "twenty billion have been 'served'."

In fact, AA's model is so flexible that the Twelve Steps have also been used as the basis for Narcotics Anonymous and to conquer other dangerous addictions, as well as to tackle compulsion and behavioral issues.

Dr. Bob and Bill W. initially started out to help themselves—two men lost in the abyss of addiction. But once they figured out how to get well, they spread the word, reaching out to cure the people once considered incurable and change the paradigm of the alcoholic's life once and for all. A potent and loving effort, run and led by alcoholics themselves, the program has spread across the globe.

Where to Begin

You might say, "What can I do to change the world? I'm just one person, with limited resources. What kind of difference can I possibly make?" Remember Anna, the eleven-year-old from the Midwest who recorded a CD and with the proceeds built two orphanages and part of a school in Haiti? Remember Aidan Hornaday dusting off his brother's harmonica, and using it to earn tens of thousands of dollars to give away to help others? And remember Bill Williams, the middle-age alcoholic with six months to live, who changed the world for thousands upon thousands of alcoholics?

None of these people looked like world changers on paper. But an eleven-year-old girl, a young boy with a harmonica, and a withering alcoholic—they're all world changers. They decided to do something, even though they had busy and difficult lives like the rest of us.

It is hard to imagine having time to research charities, much less volunteer at one. But the world probably won't be changed by a person sitting at home, "liking" a charity on Facebook or tweeting about it. Your personal engagement as a donor or volunteer is what makes your involvement meaningful. Once you have experienced that, then get back on Facebook, and "like" away or tweet to your heart's content.

As well-known author and speaker Bob Moawad said, "You can't make footprints in the sands of time by sitting on your butt. And who wants to leave buttprints in the sands of time?" To make footprints you have to step out.

Generosity Is Contagious

Generosity spreads like a very positive virus to at least three degrees of separation (from person to person to person). So consider the leverage of just one gift. For example, imagine that while having coffee with Chris, Reed explains why and how he increased his giving. Chris follows suit and tells Kara. Kara shares her enthusiasm with her friend Katie, who then also might even share the joy of giving with another, who shares with another, who shares with another. And each of those people, infected by the virus, passes it on to three others. Before you know it, we have a real movement on our hands.

> "You can't make footprints in the sands of time by sitting on your butt. And who wants to leave buttprints in the sands of time?" To make footprints you have to step out.

Where do you give? What is the need? How does it make you feel? Just talk about it. "Wow, you should see what Outreach, Inc., is doing for homeless kids in this town. It's just amazing." You're not making it about you but about the work that is being done for those who need it.

Or talk about the World-Changing Generosity movement in general; send a friend to WorldChangingGenerosity.com or give them a copy of this book. Just move the message along, and you will be leveraging your influence to save lives, fill stomachs, dig wells, educate the illiterate, remove children from slavery, house the homeless—you name it. *You* will have done it all.

How Movements Spread

Movements spread relationally, institutionally, and geographically.

Relational

- you
- family
- peers

Institutional

- church

- business
- service organizations

Geographical

- local
- national
- global

So if you decide to try this out and spread a little of the generosity virus, how do you do it? You can start by infecting every member of your family—easily, casually. Just share with them that you want to do something to help others. Let them know about something you are already doing—how cool it is be a part of a group that does great things.

Then move on to your friends and neighbors. Some of them will really *hear* you. Some will not, but that's okay. Remember, it's what you do that you're responsible for, not what they do. Those who really hear you might want more information and might eventually act. Are you shy? Don't be. All this is just conversation, not a sermon or a grand pronouncement. Remember that lives are being changed, and the mere act of you sharing your interests and concerns will unleash the power of that "group of thoughtful committed citizens" that Margaret Mead said can change the world.

Like a virus, it will take on a life of its own. You don't need to lead the movement or try to hold onto control. In fact, it's better if you don't. Just be a catalyst, and inspire people in your own sphere of influence.

> Are you shy? Don't be. All this is just conversation, not a sermon or a grand pronouncement. Remember, lives are being changed and the mere act of you sharing your interests and concerns will unleash the power of that "group of thoughtful committed citizens" that Margaret Mead said can change the world.

The Organization of a Movement

Alcoholics Anonymous founder Bill Wilson is one of the greatest examples of a catalyst behind a true movement. In the book *The Starfish and the Spider*, authors Ori Brafman and Rod A. Beckstrom refer to an open, decentralized operation like AA being like a starfish. When an arm is pulled off a starfish, another grows on. A starfish has no headquarters or CEO.

WHEN AN ARM IS PULLED OFF A STARFISH, ANOTHER GROWS ON.

In contrast, Brafman and Beckstrom compare a highly centralized operation, where control rests in a single location, to a spider. When the head is cut off a spider, it dies.

The point is we need no great central decision-making power to be generous for us or organize our efforts. In fact, decentralized outfits are among the most powerful entities in the world.

A strong example of a highly impactful decentralized approach to its mission is Wikipedia, which surrendered control of its content to users and opened the doors to contributors that today number in excess of forty-four million.

The online encyclopedia founded in 2001 is named for a wiki, a web application that allows people to add, modify, or delete content in collaboration. Instead of trying to build an encyclopedia single-handedly, Wikipedia's founders decided to let users submit and refine content. According to Wikipedia's history, "As of January 2014, Wikipedia included over 30.6 million freely useable articles in 287 languages."

What's Your Story?

For centuries, even before written language was developed, people of all colors and beliefs have shared their culture and history and passed family legacies from generation to generation to generation through storytelling.

The story of your journey of generosity might not have even begun yet. If it has, you should consider starting to record it in a journal now. As it develops, pay close attention and keep notes to capture the key points that will help you to build an effective narrative when you are ready to develop it.

You don't have to be a writer to tell your story. Just share it, as you would with a close friend. People might forget your job title, your alma mater, or even your name, but if you share it well, they won't forget your story!

Encouraging stories about others' journeys of generosity educate, inspire, and equip us to reach greater heights than we had ever imagined were possible.

To construct your story, follow this simple process:

1. For now, begin by starting to record your thoughts as notes.
2. Once you have exhausted that approach, organize your notes into outline form—from biggest idea down to details.
3. Convert your phrases into sentences in your own words and put them in an order that makes sense to you. Perhaps chronological order is easiest.
4. Have others read it and tell you if what you have written makes sense to them. If not, revise it until you feel

comfortable that the narrative you have produced sounds like you telling your story.

You can become a highly effective catalyst by sharing your story one on one or by including it on our blog at WorldChangingGenerosity.com.

If you enjoy public speaking, get out there and offer to speak to groups through a service club, church, or other group. Encourage others to do the same. A presentation can be crafted by using information, facts, and figures from this book and our website.

As you communicate your story, the impact of the three degrees of separation, explained previously, can increase the dollar value of each initial charitable gift by a whopping multiple. That could be amazing leverage, and as they say, it's just the tip of the iceberg. Imagine the potential effect of a generous giver sharing his or her heart with a large audience. How many times could each of that person's giving dollars be multiplied?

You can share your story with others by telling them

- why you give and how you give
- how you might have struggled with giving
- how your values (as a result of your faith or absence thereof) have played a role in your giving
- if you tithe, how you reached a decision to do so
- if your giving has passed beyond the tithe, how you reached a decision to do so
- if it applies, how you've learned to let go and trust God with your finances
- what impact your gifts or the gifts of others have had on specific charities and/or ministries
- how individuals' lives have been changed as a result of your gifts or the gifts of others
- whether you and your spouse are or are not in synch regarding generosity

- how you are working to establish a legacy of giving with your children (and/or grandchildren). And most importantly,
- how your heart has been transformed on your giving journey.

Tell It with Technology

The ease of twenty-first-century communication has made each of us tremendously more powerful. Today, through the use of social networks we can tell our story to thousands with the touch of a key. Twitter, Instagram, Facebook, LinkedIn, and blogs, as well as tech tools like podcasts and YouTube, have proven that we can each shape in a major way the collective opinion for the good, benefitting those who need our help.

Considering all the useless clutter on social media, wouldn't it be great to have an army of generous givers communicating about their charitable activities? We could all watch and respond to the World-Changing Generosity movement via YouTube videos and comment on a collective blog. Sweet.

Paying It Forward

Another way to spread the virus of generosity is to adopt the habit of paying it forward.

Pay it forward is more than a phrase made popular by a book and movie. The term is believed to have been coined by Lily Hammond in her 1916 book, In the Garden of Delight. It means to repay a good deed done unto you by doing something generous for the benefit of another. It is an idea so powerful that the concept was featured in a 1999 novel written by Catherine Ryan Hyde that spawned a film by the same name, released in 2000.

In the article "The Science of 'Paying It Forward'" in the New York Times Sunday Review, the author tells the story of a woman who picked up the tab for the driver next in line at a coffee shop drive-through window. The second driver did the same, as did the third. That started a three-hour chain reaction of paying it forward that impacted a total of 226 customers.

That article also reported how spontaneous generosity occurred in a sixty-seven-car chain at a Chick-fil-A restaurant and with fifty-five drivers at a Heav'nly Donuts drive-through.

The article also cites research published in the journal PLoS One. A study with six hundred participants showed that receiving and observing generosity can significantly increase a person's likelihood of being generous toward a stranger. However, while simply witnessing an act of generosity can kick off the process, it takes those who are recipients of generosity to keep it going.

The article also points out something to be wary about, which the author called the bystander effect. When people see others being extremely generous they tend to become bystanders, assuming that their help is no longer needed.

Vanessa Van Note, a blogger for the *Independent Florida Alligator*, used an analogy to explain the Pay it Forward phenomenon. She wrote, "Imagine a domino. One domino affects the outcome of one thousand dominoes. A chain reaction can begin with one person. Today, I challenge you, just as I challenge myself, to face the day with the perspective of changing the world one smile at a time, one dollar at a time, and one person at a time."

> [Pay it Forward] is believed to have been coined by Lily Hammond in her 1916 book, In the Garden of Delight. It means to repay a good deed done unto you by, instead of just thanking your benefactor, doing something generous for the benefit of another.

There are lots of ways to pay it forward. It's especially meaningful when you are actually in a position to notice someone who is short of funds. Loving a stranger who, because of you, gets to bring all the groceries home is a great feeling.

Remember that your help, if witnessed by another, can unleash a cascade of generosity that can change the world.

CHAPTER SEVEN

CREATE A GENEROUS COMMUNITY: GET INVOLVED

A community is like a ship; everyone ought to be prepared to take the helm.

—HENRIK IBSEN (1828–1906), NORWEGIAN PLAYWRIGHT, OFTEN REFERRED TO AS "THE FATHER OF REALISM"

Desperation can sometimes drive cooperation between unlikely partners.

It did so in the case of Sam Adams, then mayor of Portland, Oregon, who accepted an offer from what he considered a most unlikely and questionable source. The offer of help for Portland's troubled center city came from Kevin Palau, son of Louis Palau, an evangelist headquartered in Portland who has brought thousands to Christ. The younger Palau's idea was to address drugs, school problems, housing issues, and crime by mobilizing a group of area Christian churches to attack the city's challenges.

Mayor Adams, who is openly gay and headed a very liberal city administration, sincerely questioned whether there would be anything on which he and these conservative church leaders could agree.

SAM ADAMS, FORMER MAYOR OF PORTLAND, OREGON

Palau, who lived in a highly secular area of the country, realized that Christians were often perceived by their neighbors as folks known for being *against* things rather than *for* things. With a strong desire to change that perception, Palau and church leaders visited the mayor and posed the question, "What can we do to make a difference in Portland?"

The mayor, seeing the group's tremendous concern and sincerity, answered them honestly. He described the situation from the city's perspective as desperate, and knowing that a new approach was necessary, he accepted the group's offer to put almost 28,000 volunteers to work for the city. As a result of these conversations, during the summer of 2008, people from more than one hundred churches in the Portland area took part in hundreds of projects in the most difficult areas of the city.

By putting aside what were major, and often polarizing, philosophical differences, city officials and church volunteers came to realize that by working side by side they could accomplish feats of restoration in buildings, in neighborhoods and in the lives of some of the city's most forgotten citizens. Since that first summer, church groups have continued feeding the homeless, renovating city parks, providing foster care, countering gang violence, and counseling victims of human trafficking.

Under the auspices of CityServe Portland, churches have also begun adopting schools, running food pantries, doing yard work, conducting clothing drives, rebuilding dilapidated structures, and providing other services for their communities. Several area schools were so delighted with the results, they provided church volunteers with office space.

They called the effort the Season of Service, but Mayor Adams called it, "The largest, most successful service initiative the City of Portland has ever seen."

The impact of Season of Service has since been multiplied as volunteers from, at last count, more than five hundred churches continued to work closely with city officials and corporate leaders in a concerted annual and year-round effort to improve their community.

Community and Individual Transformation

Politics can't solve most of the problems confronting our urban areas, because each political party has its own agenda. However, the only agenda must be focused on meeting basic human needs—food for the hungry, healing for the sick, housing for the homeless, and hope for the hopeless.

When young people grow up in single-parent families that have experienced multigenerational poverty, they often feel there is no hope. To many of them, it appears to be a lot more lucrative to hold up a clerk at a convenience store than to work at a fast food outlet for $10 per hour. They consider the risk to be worth it, because they feel that they have nothing to look forward to anyway. Many end up being recruited by gangs that promote drugs, often theft, and even murder.

But hope can be found through the generous efforts of those dedicated to community transformation.

The solution to all these issues is to show people, one by one, that they matter—in fact, that they are loved. This is achieved by first taking care of basic human needs like health, food, and housing and then moving forward into mentorship, leading by example, establishing expectations that some have never before experienced, and helping with educational options that restore hope. Once those needs are met and a sense of community is developed, people are then able to reimagine a world in which their lives matter, fueling ambitions for a better life.

What Can You Do?

What does your community look like? Is it a model of generosity or are most of those with resources living in ignorance about the severity of issues that exist in their own back yards, like multigenerational poverty, homelessness, and hunger? Is yours a peaceful area, or is crime rampant? Do groups work together for the common good, or do they believe they are too far apart philosophically or theologically to collaborate?

Answer those questions and you'll see there is probably opportunity awaiting you. Remember, you don't have to lead the movement. Just light the spark. Be a catalyst.

There might be an existing group in your area you can join, or you can learn from generous community initiatives that have been put in place in cities throughout the country in an effort to transform their locales. Take ideas back to your own community and put them to work to provide a hand up to those who currently feel hopeless.

Although different approaches are being taken to transform cities and towns around the country, one similarity can be found among most of the projects already underway. The common thread is agreement that transformation requires close collaboration between government, business, education, and interfaith communities. In these cities, gone are the days when separate groups were out doing their own thing, unaware of the initiatives being undertaken by others.

In many towns and cities across the country, these groups have committed to cooperate completely and to communicate more effectively than ever before, with one goal in mind: to lift up the people who need help in their community. They have developed strategic plans that clearly define what success looks like.

Assessments are made to determine which are the greatest issues the community faces. Three or four initiatives are usually selected from issues like hunger, homelessness, education, health, job creation, violence, incarceration rate, justice, and family. Then, to achieve maximum impact, the key people involved determine how to utilize each group's strengths, including skills, training, contacts, resources, etc.

The goals of many such groups are accomplished by garnering hundreds or even thousands of laborers from volunteer sources. In a day, or in some cases a week, they serve by cleaning up neighborhoods, painting schools, or building playgrounds.

> In many towns and cities across the country, these groups have committed to cooperate completely and to communicate more effectively than ever before, with one goal in mind: to lift up the people in their community who need help.

Active community transformation efforts, projects, programs, and initiatives are being conducted throughout the country at this time. A few examples of approaches that have resulted in major results follow.

The Race in Indianapolis

If you included the word *Indianapolis* in a word association test, chances are that the immediate response would be "500." But there is another race in town—the race against poverty. In this competitive endeavor, City Mosaic is gaining substantial momentum in its attempt, through collaboration, to transform and empower people and communities in poverty.

City Mosaic envisions holistic, enduring life change that liberates individuals, rebuilds families, and revitalizes communities.

Through this effort, hundreds of area churches are now collaborating with one another, as well as with the City of Indianapolis and Indianapolis public schools, to employ a life-on-life approach to transform individual lives, beginning with immediate needs. Key initiatives are in the following areas:

- Education: Volunteers serve as mentors, tutors, and sources of encouragement for teachers, administrators, and staff.
- Affordable housing: Purchase and rehabilitate vacant and abandoned houses in target neighborhoods, making them livable and affordable for those who participate in City Mosaic's Family Transformation Initiative.
- Job creation: Entrepreneurs and skilled artisans from partner churches work with small businesses in target

neighborhoods to create meaningful job opportunities for residents and ex-offenders, who struggle with unemployment or underemployment.

- Family transformation: Volunteers commit to long-term mentoring relationships with area residents to prepare them for home ownership and to improve their health and overall stability. True family transformation strengthens individuals, families, and ultimately, the community.
- Front-line church revitalization: Training and tools are offered to enable area churches to help and empower their flocks.

For those interested in giving their time and talent, City Mosaic provides a web page where individual volunteers, contractors, bookkeepers, professionals, and others can find opportunities to serve that match their skill set and their dates and times of availability.

Indianapolis Department of Public Safety officials unveiled a report in 2014 that identified the most crime-ridden neighborhoods in the city. Understanding that true transformation cannot be achieved simply by unveiling a government program, city officials invited the faith-based community to take part. City Mosaic is at the forefront of that effort.

Big Texas Transformation

Through the Transformation West Dallas Initiative, average citizens reclaimed what was one of the most impoverished and violent urban areas in our country into what is now one of the most vibrant and safe areas in the Dallas Metroplex.

COLLABORATIVE EFFORTS CAN TRANSFORM
BLIGHTED AREAS LIKE WEST DALLAS.

Initially $500,000 was raised to purchase drug houses. Eventually, more than $10 million was pumped into the area to buy slum properties. This and other efforts resulted in the development of affordable housing, and multiple youth programs were developed in inner-city schools. City leadership then worked with the Congressional Black Caucus Scholarship Committee to award scholarships to deserving students. And, most impressively, almost two thousand formerly homeless people were moved into permanent housing, with an astounding 97 percent success rate.

This group's collaborative city transformation approach involved taking on one blighted block at a time and then moving from block to neighborhood to community to city. Areas of focus were crime reduction, neighborhood revitalization, improved education, affordable housing, jobs, and economic development.

Beginning in 2003, the initiative coordinated the efforts of more than seventy community leaders and organizations, including heads of businesses, not-for-profits, and churches, as well as the community's political leaders. The movement, which surpassed all of its original goals, continued until 2012.

An initiative of Pew Charitable Trusts, the Faith and Service Technical Education Network (FASTEN) is a treasure trove of best practice–based information for those interested in developing community transformation initiatives. FASTEN provides practical tools, informational resources, advice, and networking opportunities for those seeking to collaborate effectively to renew urban communities.

FASTEN's white papers, how-to guides, curricula, and models show faith-based organizations, public administrators (federal, state, and local), and private and corporate philanthropic foundations how to build effective cross-sector collaborations—what works and what doesn't. In addition to relationship management, community transformation organizations will find guidance in areas including start-up, volunteer management, leadership, and fundraising.

Current Initiatives

The list below is certainly not all-inclusive. More than sixty-five city transformation efforts, many of which happen to be led by either the local government or by faith-based organizations, in the following fifty-four US metropolitan areas have either taken place or are currently underway:

1. Akron, Ohio: The Love Akron Network
2. Anchorage, Alaska: The Church of Anchorage
3. Arlington, Texas: Mission Arlington / Mission Metroplex
4. Asheville, North Carolina: Revive Asheville
5. Atlanta, Georgia: One to Another
6. Austin, Texas: Austin Bridge Builders Alliance
7. Birmingham, Alabama: Mission Birmingham
8. Boise, Idaho: Treasure the Valley
9. Boston, Massachusetts: Emmanuel Gospel Center
10. Bridgeport, Connecticut: Emmaus Partnership
11. Charlotte, North Carolina: Charlotte/One

12. Chicago, Illinois: Christ Together
13. Cincinnati, Ohio: Transformation Cincinnati and Northern Kentucky
14. Cleveland, Ohio: Cleveland Hope
15. Columbia, South Carolina: Mission Columbia, Revive Columbia SC
16. Dallas, Texas: Serve West Dallas, Unite Greater Dallas, The Dallas Revival
17. Denver, Colorado: The Art of Neighboring
18. Detroit, Michigan: EACH, Motor City Makeover
19. Devils Lake, North Dakota: Revive Devils Lake
20. Durham, North Carolina: DurhamCares
21. Eugene, Oregon: One Hope
22. Flint, Michigan: Revive Flint
23. Fresno, California: ESA Love INC
24. Houston, Texas: Community Transformation Initiative, Mission Houston
25. Indianapolis, Indiana: City Mosaic
26. Kansas City, Missouri: Citywide Prayer Movement of Kansas City, Elevate KC, What if the Church?, Generosity Challenge, The Care Portal
27. Knoxville, Tennessee: Compassion Coalition
28. Lansing, Michigan: Church Of Greater Lansing
29. Little Rock, Arkansas: The Nehemiah Project
30. Long Beach, California: Hope for Long Beach
31. Louisville, Kentucky: God Transform My City
32. Miami, Florida: Mission Miami
33. Milwaukee, Wisconsin: City Transformation, Limited, Transform Milwaukee
34. Minneapolis, Minnesota: Revive Twin Cities
35. Modesto, California: Love Modesto
36. New York City, New York: New York City Leadership, Redeemer City to City
37. Olympia, Washington: Serve Thurston
38. Philadelphia, Pennsylvania: Neighborhood Transformation Initiative

39. Phoenix, Arizona: CityServe Arizona
40. Portland, Oregon: CityServe Portland
41. Prince Georges County, Maryland: Transforming Neighborhoods Initiative
42. Richmond, California, Revive Richmond CA
43. Richmond, Virginia: Boaz & Ruth
44. Rockford, Illinois: Rockford Renewal Ministries
45. San Diego, California: Vision San Diego
46. Santa Fe, New Mexico: Revive Santa Fe
47. St. Louis, Missouri: Mission Metro St. Louis
48. St. Paul, Minnesota: Revive Twin Cities
49. Seattle, Washington: Revive Seattle
50. Sedona, Arizona: Awaken the Valley
51. Stockton, California: Love Stockton
52. Tucson, Arizona: 4 Tucson
53. Utica, New York: Compassion Coalition
54. Waco, Texas: Mission Waco

Changing the World

We need to let each person know that others care, that they are loved. People are transformed one person, one heart at a time. Then we can transform neighborhoods as examples for other neighborhoods and cities as examples for other cities. Accomplishing that will enable us to heal our states as examples to other states and fix our country as an example for other countries. One by one, we can change the world.

CHAPTER EIGHT

LEAVE A LEGACY OF GENEROSITY: YOUR PASSION FOR GIVING LIVES ON

What we have done for ourselves alone dies with us; what we have done for others and the world remains and is immortal.

—ALBERT PIKE (1809–1891), AMERICAN
LAWYER, JOURNALIST, AND SOLDIER

Three boys ages seventeen, thirteen, and seven took the stage, along with their fifteen-year-old sister and grandfather. The Reeves* family had come to a meeting in Chicago to provide some insight into how younger people can be influenced by their generous elders.

Grandpa Alex began. "Since today is a school holiday, and they could be out with their friends, I really want to thank my grandchildren for giving their time to be here with me this morning, especially Tommy, the youngest, who had heart surgery last Tuesday.

"Giving has been a major part of my life for as long as I can remember. My parents were very generous and always told us kids that because we were blessed to have much compared to others in the world, we had an obligation, which was also a privilege, to give to help those who were less fortunate."

He went on to explain that when he became a father, he was determined to keep his parents' fire for giving alive by bringing his children up to appreciate how much they had and understand the joy they could realize by giving to others. And that he did.

"So, as I was signing the papers to sell a business I had started thirty-seven years before, it hit me—What am I going to do now? Then I realized that I had the opportunity to pass a legacy of giving on to my grandchildren."

One by one, Alex's grandchildren shared giving experiences that they had enjoyed with their grandfather.

The oldest boy related a story about the impact it had on him when his grandfather took him to Mexico, where they worked side by side together to build a home for an impoverished family. "The whole house wasn't even as big as our garage," he said. "Just two rooms, but this couple had never owned their own home before. I'll never forget how they broke down and cried when we handed them the keys. It was an absolutely awesome experience!"

The thirteen-year-old talked about how he and Granddad had volunteered at the local homeless shelter every Saturday for the last year. "My grandfather owned a company with seven hundred employees, but when he's at the shelter with me, he treats the men who stay there like they're just as important to him as any of the executives he used to do business with."

Alex's young granddaughter said, "Grandpa has always been the most generous man I know. He gives his time whenever anybody needs him, and he says he sees money as a tool to do good works. He has given us money to just give away at Christmas the past few years and so I think I understand how money really is a tool that can be used by all of us to help someone who needs help. Besides, giving makes me feel so happy."

Then the youngest boy, who was recovering from heart surgery, said, "I work with Granddad at the food pantry. He has volunteered there so long, he knows the names of most of the people who come in for food. He holds people's hands when he talks to them, and they know he really cares. He loves them, and it makes me so proud that I'm his grandson."

*Names have been changed

Just Do It

You have heard people say, "Life's too short." Well, that's true. Life is short, very short. So before we come abruptly to the end, it is wise to think about what kind of legacy we want to leave behind.

Who are we and how do we want to be remembered? Will the story of our lives be that we made lots of money to buy so much for our kids that they equate *things* with *love*? When we die, will our children miss us or our money? That's an awful question but one we believe that books will be written about in decades to come. We live in a culture in which cash is king, and more and more often, it is expedient to use it to buy people rather than help people.

"Just Do It" is an ad slogan that was coined in 1988 for the Nike shoe company. The "Just Do It" campaign was so successful that during the next decade it pushed the company's share of the North American domestic sport-shoe market from 18 percent to 43 percent, from $877 million to $9.2 billion in worldwide sales.

Why did it have such an amazing impact? Because it made athletes question all the excuses they used to avoid getting out there to exercise, run, lift, or whatever reason they bought Nike shoes for in the first place.

It was powerful because excuses need to be examined. The challenge now is to examine your own. To make headway in life, as in sport, we need to move past *why we can't* and get to *why we can*. Your legacy is worth the effort.

> *The moment of truth—the sudden emergence of a new insight—is an act of intuition. It may be likened to an immersed chain, of which only the beginning and the end are visible … the diver vanishes at one end and comes up at the other, guided by invisible links.*
>
> —ARTHUR KOESTLER (1905–1983) BRITISH NOVELIST

Interestingly, legacies are usually not built by concentrating on how we'll look to future generations. They are built by concentrating on finding ways to help others. Such is the story of Don Schoendorfer. A top engineer in the health care industry, he was directed by an inner force into a life of amazing service.

The Woman on the Road

Schoendorfer was perfectly equipped to compete in the expansive economic times of the past three decades. Armed with a PhD in mechanical engineering from MIT and an undergraduate degree from Columbia, he worked his way up to head research and development at companies like Haemonetics and Baxter Healthcare.

But on a vacation to Morocco in the 1970s an event he witnessed planted a vision in his mind that he could not forget. As he stood by the side of a Moroccan thoroughfare, he saw a woman dodging traffic, pulling herself with her fingertips to drag her body across the road.

Time and life passed quickly, but years later, the image was still as vivid as the day he saw her. He knew it was time to work on the problem of getting wheelchairs to people like her. Even used chairs can cost hundreds to revamp and ship, he reasoned. Also, he knew that in developing countries, the terrain was too rough and standard wheelchair parts too delicate for the conditions they would encounter; repair parts would be impossible to find and the chairs too expensive to distribute globally. There had to be a better way.

Schoendorfer began tinkering with a design that was brilliant in its simplicity. He used a white plastic lawn chair, bicycle tires, and other parts that can be found in most parts of the world and easily replaced if necessary. The chairs were tough, cheap, and easily repairable. So he set to work.

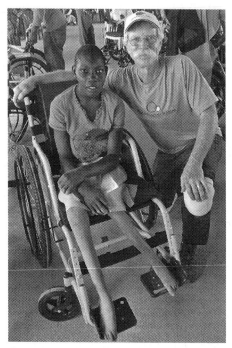

DON SCHOENDORFER GIVES THE GIFT OF FREEDOM AND
INDEPENDENCE TO PEOPLE AROUND THE WORLD.

After building the first one hundred wheelchairs in his garage, he learned about a short-term medical mission to India sponsored by his church. The team was looking for doctors and nurses to do basic field medicine in rural India, not engineers with unproven inventions. "I buffaloed my way into the whole program," he recalls. "Nobody could understand how this was going to work. They humored me and allowed me to bring four of my wheelchairs along."

As the team worked at a clinic in Chennai, a Hindu family arrived. They had carried their eleven-year-old son, who was stricken with cerebral palsy, more than three kilometers for help. When the mother saw Schoendorfer's wheelchair, she placed her son in it and started to push him around the waiting area of the makeshift clinic. The boy who had to be moved to go to the bathroom, the boy who had to be carried if he ever left the house, was suddenly free. It was as if someone had taken the lock off a prison door and said, "Go ahead. You can leave."

Schoendorfer's Free Wheelchair Mission estimates that there are up to a hundred million people in the world who need wheelchairs. Accordingly, their approach is straightforward: to design the least expensive wheelchair possible and distribute as many as possible.

Today, the wheelchairs have been delivered to some of the most remote areas of the globe, transforming the quality of life for not only the afflicted individuals but for their families as well. For them, receiving a wheelchair is a life-transforming experience; it means not only the opportunity for access, employment, education, and health care but provides gifts vital to the human spirit—independence, dignity, and hope.

The Free Wheelchair Mission is currently active in ninety-one countries and has distributed more than 781,000 wheelchairs, touching everyone they meet with the gift of love. Said Schoendorfer, "We've given wheelchairs to people who haven't been out of their rooms for thirty years."

Is anyone who has ever heard of Don Schoendorfer going to see him as a health care engineer? Or will he always be, in the view of his family, friends, and the world, the man who started the Free Wheelchair Mission, the man who changed the world for thousands who, if not for him, could only crawl or be carried.

There is no way to measure success like this. No way to count the lives touched by one person's reaction to another's need or pain. It is a starfish story, like all the stories in this book: a story about people working to give others a chance, which always, always gives birth to a legacy that affects the giver and his or her family in amazing and powerful ways.

Considering the people you've met through these pages, do you think the story of their lives will be anything more than one you have read about? Do you think their kids will not always remember and pass on the things their parents did for others as the salient points of their lives? They will. For sure they will. Because more important than the estate you pass on is the legacy of love and generosity you leave behind.

There is so much more to life than a checkbook. And the way to find that out and experience the way of the generous giver is to Just Do It.

Legacy Planning

If you are a planner and like to have things down on paper, this information is for you. If you are a person who just likes to dive in, that's fine too. But those who want to *plan* a legacy should know planning is just the first step. The next steps include sharing those plans, as well as your values and life experiences, in the form of a story.

Some of the greatest families of givers we know have legacy stories and plans in place. The whole family is on board, and this adds to their power and effectiveness as generosity machines— planning, working, and enjoying the journey together.

Planning a personal or family legacy can start with developing a charitable philosophy, which is a document that describes why you believe you or your family have been able to acquire wealth, how much you should retain, what you intend to do with what you keep, how much you should give away and to whom.

If you have a spouse, it is essential that you are in agreement about your charitable philosophy. If you do not agree, iron out any wrinkles before trying to influence younger members of the family in any way. Imagine how traffic would flow with conflicting signals. Children and grandchildren will immediately detect dissension, and the focus will be taken off the essential idea of giving.

If religious teaching plays a part in your motivation to give, you should obviously make prayer a part of every step of this process. If you are a spiritual family, citing related passages from your faith's guiding book strengthens your message.

Consider putting your family's story in writing. Providing a permanent record will be useful as a map for future generations to fall back upon.

Raising Generous Children

Be careful not to become frustrated with younger members of your family because they do not seem to grasp what you believe is important in life. Remember that they are growing up in an environment of consumerism. Be generously patient with them, consistently providing the understanding that they need.

GRANDPARENTS ARE IN A POWERFUL POSITION TO LEAD
GRANDCHILDREN ON THE PATH OF A GENEROUS LIFE.

Make it your role to teach younger members of your family what generosity is all about. One of the most effective ways to learn is to experience something together. So volunteering with your children or grandchildren is a good approach. Taking them on a mission trip to another country, where they'll see poverty at a level they'll never experience in the United States, can make a long-lasting impact on their hearts.

Some parents have turned what has always been spring break on the beach into a mission trip. If you do so, you might also consider letting each child invite a friend to come along, making it a fun learning experience that will undoubtedly produce the first of many stories in their own long and generous lives. A less expensive approach is a stay-cation—time off without going away—in which you could volunteer together at a local charity or at several charities.

> Volunteering with your children or grandchildren is a good approach. Taking them on a mission trip to another country, where they'll see poverty at a level they'll never experience in the United States, can make a long-lasting impact on their hearts.

Holidays create another opportunity to share the joy of giving with your children or grandchildren. Many people we know use Thanksgiving as a teaching opportunity by giving each child some money to donate to a charity or person in need. Each child's Christmas present to their parents or grandparents is to explain who received the help and how it made the child feel by writing about it or producing a simple video that he or she shoots on a smart phone. The amount can be $10 or $100 or more. The experience is far more important than the amount.

Opening a Donor Advised Fund, or DAF, for children or grandchildren would also enable them to learn what it's like to give money away, also giving you an opportunity to discuss the experience with them, including why they selected a charity and how they felt about it afterwards. You can even offer to match whatever they donate.

You can invite missionaries or others who dedicate their lives to charitable purposes to stay at your home and, after dinner, share stories about their work. Another idea is to have a birthday party; ask guests bring presents to be taken to a children's shelter and deliver them together.

Your Financial Finish Line

As you round the bend into the last half of your years on this planet, you need to come to a conclusion about what your finish line is: that is, how much you need to accumulate to see you and, if married, your spouse through the remainder of your lives.

Then you need to ask the $64,000 question: how much do we leave the kids?

Although many believe that money is to be accumulated and divided among their children, dumping a trailer-load of money on your kids is not usually wise when you are considering their happiness over a lifetime.

We've all heard about young people inheriting so much that they never had to work another day in their lives. Too often we hear horror stories about how they turned to alcohol, drugs, or some other destructive lifestyle. But even if members of your family would never take so negative a path, the danger of children and grandchildren living off their elders' life energy (which is what money actually is) is dangerous in itself.

Simply put, you should consider how much is enough to provide your children with a leg up in life, but not so much that they won't have to earn their own way.

At one time, the most common occupation in our country was farming. The primary inheritance a farmer left for his children was land, the acreage that was necessary to produce the food needed to feed one's family. Inheritors of the land still had to plant, reap, and work. As centuries have passed, there are fewer and fewer family farms in our country. What we can give our children now to give them the ability to make a living is an education.

Beyond that, how much is enough? How much is too much? These are the questions that you need to answer.

If you've ever heard the adage "shirtsleeves to shirtsleeves in three generations," you might wonder what it means.

Shirtsleeves to Shirtsleeves

Interestingly, this universal proverb is as old as writing itself, and it appears in every culture: clogs to clogs, kimono to kimono, rice paddy to rice paddy, shirtsleeves to shirtsleeves. The proverb describes the oft-traveled path of failure for once-prosperous families.

The theory of the proverb is that the first generation starts off in a rice paddy. Two people with an affinity for one another come together, struggle, build wealth, and create a financial fortune. They usually do it without making significant changes to their values, customs, or lifestyle. The second generation inherits the wealth, moves to the city, puts on beautiful clothes, joins the opera board, runs big organizations, and then the fortune plateaus. The third generation, with no work experience, consumes the remainder of the financial pie, and it's back to the rice paddy. This is the classic formulation of the shirtsleeves proverb, which is as true today as it has been throughout evolved human history.

And the proverb is borne out by statistics. According to the *Wall Street Journal*, 70 percent of families waste away their wealth in generation two, and 90 percent of families end up with little or nothing from the inheritance they received as a result of their grandparents' financial success.

> Interestingly, this universal proverb is as old as writing itself. And it appears in every culture: clogs to clogs, kimono to kimono, rice paddy to rice paddy, shirtsleeves to shirtsleeves. The proverb describes the path of failure for prosperous families.

Family Culture

At one time, long before newspapers, radio, television, computers, and smart phones, families sat around the fire at night, and stories were passed from one generation to the next. Older members of the family shared their values and told stories that painted a crystal-clear picture of who their family was and what the family name stood for, laced with many examples of obstacles faced and overcome to preserve their legacy.

Today, many families are unable to even share a meal together without the interference of texting, much less share a conversation with each other.

Legacy-minded people, on the other hand, are vigilant in raising their children and planning their estates in a way that will most benefit their progeny. It starts with bringing up children in loving, caring homes. It continues with training in compassion for others and being generous with money and time, at all times leading by example. It involves instructions to work hard in school and at jobs, with an emphasis on expectations and personal responsibility.

A critical element in leaving a legacy of generosity is sharing stories that clearly illustrate the importance of the family's values.

Reading a Need

Lucile Heppner's family lived near a small, rather unprosperous town. As she told the story, they had no library, and most families had no books.

She knew a library was needed—a project requiring both money and a referendum. So a vote was taken, and the ballot box was literally on her front porch. Lucile lobbied the owner of the local newspaper, she called folks she knew would support the plan out to vote, and she led the fundraising effort. She is also named on a plaque in the library to this day.

Lucile died shortly after her 101st birthday. She accomplished so much, both privately and publicly. But what she told her grandchildren about over and over was the time she started the library.

Her children wanted readers of her obituary to understand what a big part of Lucile's life the founding of the library had been.

101

Look at the obituaries on any given day. The children of the dear departed don't tout the money the person made or what a fancy car they drove, but how generous he or she was in their time here on earth. It is the stuff of legacy, where the rubber meets the road, a "this is how great they were" kind of statement that defines them as the most human of human beings.

Succession Planning

As you age, don't forget to consider preparing your heir apparent to continue to lead the family (and the family business if applicable) once you are gone. A lack of attention here will greatly diminish whatever impact you were able to make during your entire lifetime.

To leave a true legacy of generosity, you can't just talk about it; you need to live it and to lead by example. Be careful; it's not all about money. Generosity is also about how you treat others—with respect, recognizing the uniqueness of others—and it includes giving freely of your time and talent. Remember, it's not the valuables you leave behind that are important. It's the values.

PART III: GENEROSITY AS A VALUE

Gentleness, self-sacrifice and generosity are the exclusive possession of no one race or religion.

—MAHATMA GANDHI (1869–1948), WHO EMPLOYED NONVIOLENT CIVIL DISOBEDIENCE TO BECOME THE PREEMINENT LEADER OF INDIAN NATIONALISM IN BRITISH-RULED INDIA

Understanding the Thought Groups

What drives us to even consider a generous life in the first place? What shapes our attitudes and, subsequently, our behavior?

Most would agree that we form our beliefs based on our values. Our values translate into our virtues, our moral and ethical principles, which greatly impact our ideals, what we think is important, how we behave, and how we want to be viewed by others.

Many peoples' values are shaped by their or their parents' religion or the absence of religious influence. Religion or the absence thereof can determine worldview that affects the way in which people interact with others and with their environment.

Although many say there is no difference in the level of generosity between those who are religious and those who aren't, there is research that contradicts this assertion.

A study released by the *Chronicle of Philanthropy* in 2012, based on Internal Revenue Service records of those who itemized deductions in 2008, shows that states where religious participation is higher than the rest of the country gave the greatest percentage of discretionary income to charity. Conversely, states with the least religiously affiliated populace gave the lowest percentage of their income to charity.

> Interestingly, every group linked by a set of beliefs, be it religious or decidedly nonreligious — *every single one* promotes generosity.

Also published in 2012 in an edition of *Social Psychological and Personality Science Journal* is a study that says just the opposite.

It concludes that less religious people are more compassionate and generous than highly religious people. Conducted at UC Berkeley in California, it is actually a combination of three separate studies. First, in a 2004 national survey, 1,300 American adults were included. Second, 101 American adults were questioned. And more than 200 college students were involved in the third.

The *Chronicle of Philanthropy* study was based on tax records, while the UC Berkeley study was a collection of surveys composed of self-reported behavior. The nonreligious point out that a large portion of religious giving is to churches, which they don't consider charity, but religious people believe that their churches allocate a major portion of their time and budgets to charitable works within their membership, in their neighborhoods, their states, throughout the United States, and around the world.

So you can see there is no end to the debate about members of which thought group give more, care more, or do more. Interestingly, every group linked by a set of beliefs, be it religious or decidedly nonreligious, promotes generosity. Could it be more obvious that a concept this widespread is part and parcel of our makeup as human beings?

In the following chapters we will share with you what major religions teach their followers and how the nonreligious look at generosity. The top-ten US groups are presented in descending order, based on the estimated numbers of followers that each has in the United States. Also included, where applicable, are estimated worldwide numbers.

CHAPTER NINE

CHRISTIANITY: 224.4 MILLION IN THE UNITED STATES (2.1 BILLION WORLDWIDE)

For where your treasure is, there your heart will be also.

—JESUS (MATTHEW 6:21), WRITTEN BY
MATTHEW, ONE OF TWELVE DISCIPLES OF JESUS

Katherine is a Christian, a follower of Jesus, who is known for her love for her neighbors. She had an accident that left her with a hip broken into so many pieces that she now has two rods in it and walks slowly, with a pronounced limp.

In spite of that, she continues to rise early in the morning to go to work every day at a bakery. Katherine says that although the bakery sells bread, she knows that some people come specifically because they have prayer requests, so she always makes time to pray for them.

One day, when she and a customer, Debbie, were talking, Katherine mentioned that she was saving for a better car, because she was constantly paying for expensive car repairs. She said that she had been saving money but it would take a few years to save enough.

A few months later, when Debbie came into the bakery, she asked Katherine how her car fund was coming along. Katherine paused, took a deep breath, and answered, "I gave it all away. There was a widow who was desperate with children to feed, and I gave her the five thousand dollars I had saved."

Debbie was shocked. Katherine, who had so little, gave it all away because she met somebody she believed needed the money more than she did.

That evening, Debbie told her husband about Katherine. She had made up her mind to help, but she needed to get her husband on board. She looked into his eyes and said, "Pete, I think we need to help Katherine with her car fund."

Pete studied his wife's face and shook his head. "No," he said. "We need to buy Katherine a car."

That night, he called their friend Scott, who was the owner of a car dealership, and asked him if he knew Katherine at the bakery. He explained that he and his wife would like to buy her a car.

"That's great!" said Scott. "New or used?"

Pete thought, *Why would he ask me that? A used car would certainly be good enough.* But that's not what Pete said. He paused for a moment and answered, "I want a new car." Scott, moved by his friend's gesture, said, "A new car? Okay. If you're going to do that, I want to help."

Meanwhile, Debbie found out that Katherine had been saving for an SUV, so the group bought a new SUV and arranged to deliver it the next day. Both families showed up at the bakery and walked Katherine outside to present her with her new vehicle.

Katherine was overcome with emotion. Weeping and smiling, she said, "For me? This is for me? I knew that God had many cars, but I didn't know that he had a new one for me." They all stood there in tears as they witnessed the joy on Katherine's face and shared the experience together.

Debbie hugged Katherine and whispered that they would like the gift to be confidential, but Debbie says she keeps running into people who say, "I heard what you did for Katherine!"

Says Debbie, "It wasn't even us. It was Katherine who started it all, giving up all she had saved to help the widow in the first place. And it continues on. Generosity begets generosity."

"We don't give in order to receive," said Katherine, wiping away her tears. "We give because it's the nature of Jesus Christ. He gave us His life."

The Christian Culture of Giving

Katherine, who had little, gave all the money she had saved to the widow for whom she had compassion. Katherine's treasure followed her heart. Debbie's and Pete's hearts were captured by Katherine, and you know the rest of the story.

The words in the verse at the beginning of this chapter, "For where your treasure is, there your heart will be also," are found in the New Testament of the Bible, in the book of Matthew, chapter 6, verse 21. They are the words of Jesus Christ (6–2 BC to AD 29–30) whose life and teachings during his final three years on Earth formed the basis for Christianity.

STAINED GLASS WINDOW DEPICTING JESUS
NANCY BAUER / SHUTTERSTOCK.COM

Christians believe that Jesus is the Son of God and that He is one with God, Creator of the universe, who came to earth in human form. After He gave His life, He left the world the Holy

Spirit that continues to dwell within each Christian. Father, Son, and Holy Spirit are not three beings. They are the one triune God.

Jesus said that His followers would be known by their love for Him and for each other. He instructed them to show their love by giving their time, talent, and treasure to provide aid to the poor, widows, orphans, and the downtrodden.

The word *give* appears 921 times in the Bible, almost as many times as *faith* (270), *hope* (165), and *love* (541) combined. Generosity-related topics are referenced more than any other subject in the Bible—two times more than *heaven* and *hell* combined, three times more than *love*, seven times more than *prayer*, and eight times more than *belief*. Seventeen of the thirty-eight parables told by Jesus relate to giving. The Bible includes more than 2,300 verses on the subject.

> The word *give* appears 921 times in the Bible, almost as many times as *faith* (270), *hope* (165), and *love* (541) added together.

Most Christians consider tithing to mean giving 10 percent off the top of their income. In the Old Testament (Deuteronomy 14:23, Malachi 3: 8–9, Malachi 3:11, Leviticus 27–30, Proverbs 3:9–10), giving this sum to the church was stressed heavily. What many don't realize is that there were actually *three* different tithes mentioned in the Old Testament (Leviticus 27:30–33; Numbers 18:21–32; Deuteronomy 12:6, 14:22–29, 26:12), which would represent a total of 23.3 percent:

1. a tithe to be paid to the church
2. a tithe to spend on the household and friends to remind them of God's love of generosity
3. a triannual tithe (given every three years)

However, in the New Testament, Jesus said that His followers should give whatever they could give cheerfully (2 Corinthians 9:7), which some interpret to mean that whatever you decide, even if less than a tithe, is fine. But others believe that He intended that giving be even greater than the Old Testament tithes and that those who gave at that level should be delighted to do it. After all, his twelve disciples gave up everything they had to follow Jesus.

An intriguing verse in Malachi 3:10 says, "'Bring the whole tithe into the storehouse that there may be food in my house. Test me in this,' says the Lord Almighty, 'and see if I will not throw open the floodgates of heaven and pour out so much blessing that there will not be room enough to store it.'"

Christian scripture teaches that Almighty God created the universe and everything in it; He owns it all. Christians are simply stewards of the wealth He has bestowed upon them during this life on earth. In Ephesians 2:6, 1 Peter 2:11, Hebrews 11:13, Hebrews 13:14, and Philippians 3:20, Christians are told that they are aliens here; heaven, not earth, is their home; they need to think eternally, not temporally.

"Bring the whole tithe into the storehouse that there may be food in my house. Test me in this," says the Lord Almighty, "and see if I will not throw open the floodgates of heaven and pour out so much blessing that there will not be room enough to store it."

Matthew 6:19–20 records Jesus's words: "Do not store up for yourselves treasures on earth where moth and rust destroy, and where thieves break in and steal. But store up for yourselves treasures in Heaven, where moth and rust do not destroy, and where thieves do not break in and steal." Or, as Pastor Randy Alcorn says in his book *The Treasure Principle*, "You can't take it with you—but you can send it on ahead."

CHAPTER TEN

NON-THEISTS: 40.3 MILLION IN THE UNITED STATES (1.1 BILLION WORLDWIDE)

This category includes agnosticism, atheism, free thought, Humanism, secular humanism, secularism, and skepticism. Although there are distinct beliefs unique to some of these groups and others claim an absence of any belief system, the common thread is that they either reject religious belief or are indifferent to religion.

> *Generosity goes far beyond organized charity, of course. We must also model the kind of generosity of spirit that improves everyone's experience of daily life.*
>
> —Dale McGowan, *Parenting Beyond Belief: On Raising Ethical, Caring Kids without Religion*

Multiple news stories have been published about Robert W. Wilson—philanthropist, tremendously successful stock market investor, and retired hedge-fund manager—who funded a scholarship program for disadvantaged inner-city students.

Gifts are made to private schools almost every day. What made this one so newsworthy? It wasn't just that in 2007 Wilson gave the Archdiocese of New York the largest donation it had ever received: $22.5 million. It wasn't just that the then eighty-year-old was not even Catholic. It was, most surprisingly, the fact that he happened to be a self-proclaimed atheist.

By the time he was eighty-three, Wilson's total donations to inner-city Catholic education topped $30 million.

Why in the world would an atheist support an arm of the

Roman Catholic Church? Wilson explained that the way he saw it, his money was going to fund scholarships to pay tuition for the students. It was about giving these young people choices to get out of underperforming schools into good ones. More than half of the students enrolled in New York's Catholic schools were living below the federal poverty line.

As often happens, Wilson's giving fueled even more generosity. After his gift was announced, an anonymous donor gave an additional $4.5 million.

This overflowing wave of generosity followed a time period of declining donations that had forced closure of some Catholic schools.

The head of the archdiocese, Cardinal Edward Egan, didn't refuse to accept Wilson's $22.5 million charitable contribution because it came from an atheist. When Cardinal Egan and Wilson met, they discovered that they not only shared a love for the young beneficiaries of these scholarships but for opera as well.

On PhilanthropyRoundtable.org, Wilson is quoted as saying, "I remember the first time I had lunch with Cardinal Egan. We were finishing up, and he said, 'Well, now that you've given all this money to our schools, I should try to convert you.' I said to him, 'Well, Cardinal, if you do, I suppose I should try to convert you. The only problem is that if I succeed, you'll lose your job.'"

In 2006, with $147.2 million in charitable gifts, Wilson was the twelfth-most generous donor in the United States, according to the *Chronicle of Philanthropy*.

In an interview with the Associated Press the year before his gift to the archdiocese, Wilson said that his goal was to give away 70 percent of his $500-million fortune before he died.

How did Robert Wilson become so generous? Since he is now deceased, we can't know for sure, but more than likely it was part of his upbringing. While conducting research, we ran across a book that emphasizes the importance of the value of generosity being passed on to younger generations today.

The quote at the beginning of this chapter was found in Dale McGowan's book, *Parenting Beyond Belief.* Chapter five of that book, *Values and Virtues, Meaning and Purpose,* includes what McGowan calls "Seven Secular Virtues," which include humility, empathy, courage, honesty, openness, generosity, and gratitude. An emphasis on empathy is a thread that runs throughout the book. The author asks parents to push the envelope by exposing children to other neighborhoods, areas, and countries so they experience poverty up close and learn that compassion is expected to result in generosity.

"We don't need God to be good," is a commonly used slogan among the nonreligious. In fact, the tagline below the logo of one of the non-theist thought groups, American Humanist Association, is an adaptation of this quote. It is, "Good Without a God."

Generosity plays a key role in Humanism, as it does in many of the other nonreligious thought groups. They believe that only humans can provide solutions to human problems, and they have historically been quietly involved in many social causes and charities.

> Generosity plays a key role in Humanism, as it does in many of the other nonreligious thought groups. They believe that only humans can provide solutions to human problems and have historically been quietly involved in many social causes and charities.

Although those in America with no religious affiliation have made up the fastest-growing group since 2008, according to a 2012 Gallup survey that growth slowed significantly during 2012. Within this group, the eighteen- to twenty-year-olds surveyed made up the study's largest subgroup. They are three times as likely to be unaffiliated with religion as senior citizens are.

According to a 2012 Pew Research Center report, nearly two out of three American adults under thirty are affiliated with a faith tradition, compared with four out of five American adults overall.

Many of the unaffiliated are quick to point out that several of America's most generous philanthropists are nonbelievers. Take for example self-described agnostics Warren Buffett, Bill Gates, and Melinda Gates. According to *Forbes,* regarding the *Forbes 400: The Richest People in America* 2012 issue, "Pals Gates and Buffett are the most generous people on the planet, having given $28 billion and $17.5 billion to date, respectively ..." And since that time, Buffett has pledged another $3 billion: $1 billion to each of the charitable foundations of his three children. The Richard Dawkins Foundation for Reason and Science confirms the $28 billion in lifetime giving for Gates but claims that Buffett has donated almost $41 billion. The foundation also includes Hungarian-American business magnate and investor George Soros, at almost $7 billion.

The three studies cited in the beginning of this section of the book conducted by researchers at the University of California, Berkeley, show that nonreligious people perform acts of generosity more from feelings of compassion than do religious people, who give based on doctrine and out of a desire to please their god. These studies show that, for the nonreligious, the strength of their emotional connection to another person is critical to whether or not they will help that person.

CHAPTER ELEVEN

JUDAISM: 4 MILLION IN THE UNITED STATES (17 MILLION WORLDWIDE)

A generous person will become rich, and he who sates [others] shall himself become sated as well.

—MISHLEI (PROVERBS 11:25)

Zane Buzby—dubbed "the female Robin Williams" by *People* magazine—had made it. From rural Wisconsin to the movie and TV stages of LA, Zane Buzby had become a Hollywood player.

A generation before, her Russian Jewish grandfather had landed the family in northern Wisconsin and named her after one of his favorite authors: Zane Grey, who wrote stories of cowboys and conquests.

Show business success yielded perks; Zane had both the money and time to travel. So in 2001, at her mother's urging, she decided to visit the Lithuanian villages where her grandmothers had been born. Says Zane, "I thought I was going to take a few pictures for my sister and my mom, report back to the family, and go on with my life."

On one of her first days there she met David Katz, who had founded an organization to help Jewish World War II survivors. They struck up a friendship, and before she left, Katz gave her a list of eight elderly survivors who "hadn't had a visitor in God knows how long." He simply told her that they were old and alone and asked her to visit them.

Buzby agreed.

She hired a translator, drove through a labyrinth of country roads, and started knocking on the doors of shabby, disintegrating wooden huts. She found aged men and women in their back yards digging potatoes in the cold weather, hoping to save them before they froze in the ground. They were in their eighties and nineties and had struggled since the Holocaust to have enough food to survive and enough money to buy the most basic medical treatment.

On the flight home, Buzby couldn't get the faces of those she had met off her mind and vowed to help. Today, she oversees a network of support for a wide assemblage of elderly Jews—most the sole survivors of their families, or even of their entire villages. Many of them were escapees from the Einsatzgruppen, the German paramilitary squads charged with the massacre of the Jewish population in occupied Soviet lands.

The Catch-22 for these survivors is that because they avoided deportation to a concentration camp or ghetto, most are ineligible for Holocaust compensation from the German government and don't qualify for regular financial aid from major Jewish organizations.

"My pension allows me to buy only bread and milk, and I am already an old and ill person," Raisa Kivovna, from the Ukraine, wrote in a letter to Buzby. "My legs almost don't work; I practically crawl around the apartment ... I have been accustomed to hunger since childhood and wanted, at least in old age, to live in a human way."

The Survivor Mitzvah Project that Buzby started now supplies Raisa and other elderly Holocaust survivors in remote villages with direct financial aid, along with desperately needed food, medicine, and suitable shelter and a big helping of loving kindness. Many fought with the Russians or were slaves in the Gulag long after the war ended. They are alone and isolated and receive little or no monetary assistance aside from the money they receive from this charity's efforts.

It isn't all about money. Zane corresponds with more than two thousand of these recipients, with help from three part-time employees and a volunteer Russian translator. She has received more than ten thousand letters over the years, which she dutifully keeps for posterity, along with pictures of many with worn, wrinkled faces whose eyes tell a story of a pained and wanting life.

Zane Buzby, named after the author of stories of cowboys and conquests, has written a story of her own. It is the story of the conquest of self, of tremendous generosity, personal sacrifice, and love for her fellow man.

Based on the teachings of her people, Zane Buzby's caring and her generous spirit are no surprise. From the origination of Judaism, under Abraham (2018–1843 BC) and Moses (1391–1271 BC), these values have been passed on from generation to generation.

FRESCO OF MOSES BY JOSEPH SCHONMAN, 1857
RENATA SEDMAKOVA / SHUTTERSTOCK.COM

They are part of the Torah, the Jewish name for the first five books of the Hebrew bible, which contain laws given to Moses by God. They are included in the Tanakh, known to non-Jews as the Old Testament, which is the entire body of Jewish teachings and law. The same is true of the Talmud, an expression of Judaism's Oral Law, as well as an explanation of the Tanakh.

In the Torah, Jews learn that charity begins at home in their own community, but it is not to be limited to their own kind. It also must be an act done willingly from the heart; sacrificial giving will be rewarded more highly than only giving what is comfortable. It is better to provide a way for the poor to make a living than to just give them handouts. There will always be poor, and giving to them is just giving back what belongs to God.

The Tanakh also sets out many protections for the poor. For example, the poor are not to be taken advantage of when they are indebted to a Jew. Jews started out as nomadic shepherds wandering in the wilderness. Then they became farmers and later urban dwellers, some of whom became very wealthy. Wealth is good, as long as it is used to do good. So wealth became highly valued in the Tanakh.

Charity is a foundational element of Jewish life. Giving at least 10 percent of income to charity is common for traditional Jews. They make charitable donations to express thanks to God, to ask His forgiveness, or to ask for His favor. In effect, Jews replaced the act of honoring God through animal sacrifice, common in the first century, with the practice of honoring God through charitable donations.

Helping the less fortunate has always been an obligation under Jewish law. So everybody in the community contributed to a collection box. The *kuppah*, or poor box, was commonly found in synagogues. Jews placed contributions into it at weekly services, as well as for joyful and sad occasions. Author Paul Johnson writes in *In a History of the Jews*, "From Temple times, the kuppah, or collecting box, was a pivot around which the Jewish welfare community revolved."

It was the ultimate safety net for Jews, who often lived

in poverty. Kuppah funds were used to feed the poor, to bury them, even as the dowry for girls from poor families. Givers and recipients remained anonymous.

In Jewish life, a beggar is considered to be doing the giver a favor by providing the opportunity to exercise what Jews call *tzedakah*, which is synonymous with charity, but Jews don't view tzedakah as generosity. It means righteousness, fairness, and justice and is considered to be an obligatory form of giving that doesn't require the heart to be moved in any way. It is the performance of a duty, including taking care of your children beyond the age of legal requirement and giving to support Gentile as well as Jewish causes.

Tzedakah is to be practiced joyfully, indicating compassion or empathy with those in sorrow, a celebration of the opportunity to share in the Almighty's work.

Eight Levels of Charity

Maimonides, a twelfth century Jewish sage, defined eight levels of tzedakah, each higher than the preceding one. They are, from the lowest level to the highest level, as follows:

8. giving grudgingly
7. giving not enough, but cheerfully
6. giving directly to the poor, but only when asked
5. giving directly to the poor without being asked
4. giving when you don't know the recipient but he knows your identity
3. giving when you know the recipient but he does not know your identity
2. giving when neither knows the identity of the other (i.e., communal funds administered by a third party)
1. helping someone to become self-sufficient before he or she becomes impoverished so that future charity won't be needed

In addition to giving from riches, it is also acceptable to give time or wisdom. The key is for Jews to make giving and kindness the essences of one's being.

Jews believe that, by practicing generosity, they receive blessings on four levels:

- physical: A place to congregate as a community
- emotional: A sense of belonging
- intellectual: A genuine sense of integrity
- spiritual: God's presence in our lives, wealth from the Divine

Jews who attended Hebrew school first associated tzedakah, the Hebrew word loosely understood to mean charity, with the *pushke*—a small metal box that was given to students, with instructions to collect pennies in the pushke to plant trees in Israel. Today, many say that *tikkun olam,* meaning to repair the world, guides their giving.

CHAPTER TWELVE

ISLAM: 1.6 MILLION IN THE UNITED STATES (1.5 BILLION WORLDWIDE)

They feed with food—despite their own desire for it—the indigent, and the orphan and the captive (saying): "We feed you purely for the sake of God. We desire no reward from you, nor thankfulness.

—SURAH AL-INSAN 8–9

The Muslim Consultative Network (MCN) is a New York City–based organization of more than 150 Muslims who help prepare and serve food to low-income and homeless New Yorkers at the Holy Trinity Church Soup Kitchen.

The staff and volunteers of MCN spent the tenth anniversary of 9/11 preparing three hundred bagged lunches to ultimately be distributed around the city to those in need. During that time the group also participated in the annual Children of Abraham Peace Walk and arranged children's workshops to make thank-you cards for volunteer firemen.

"During the walk, the children presented their cards and gifts to the firemen in appreciation for putting their lives at risk on September 11, 2001," says MCN Board Chair Debbie Almontaser.

Across the river in New Jersey, Mashal Anjum organizes a major fundraising event with the Thaakat Foundation, a nonprofit aimed at promoting charitable giving and volunteerism among students and young professionals alike. She strives to raise enough money to build a school for impoverished Pakistani children who live in a trash dump.

"The people living there are so poor that they burn garbage, and research finds that burning garbage releases a dangerous chemical known as dioxin, which causes terrible respiratory problems," explains Anjum. "The villagers want their children to go to school, but the school is too close to where the garbage is burned, so Thaakat is raising funds to build a school a mile away from the village."

Thaakat initiatives serve people irrespective of religion or race, but like the volunteers at MCN, Anjum's charitable giving is motivated by her commitment to Islam.

"I personally believe that I will be asked by God what I did with my time and resources, of which we are so blessed. It cannot be random that a person like me is given so much compared to a mother and her many children, all of whom are going to sleep hungry," articulates Anjum. "I believe that some people are sent to this world to do good for others, and that is our test."

Islam and the Qur'an

Much of what Mashal Anjum expressed above is reflected in the Qur'an, which is regarded by Muslims as the word of God and the basis for the religion of Islam, founded about AD 622.

The Qur'an says that Allah, or God, who is Al Kareem, the Most Generous, knows the hearts of men, and He will replace whatever a person generously gives away with the intention of pleasing Him.

Followers of Islam believe that everything originates from God and everything will return to Him. So it is logical to behave as if everything they possess is merely a loan, something they, as stewards, have an obligation to preserve, protect, and ultimately share.

The Qur'an is believed to have been passed down over a period spanning twenty-three years in the form of messages directly from Allah through the angel Gabriel to Islam's founder, Prophet Muhammad (AD 570–632). He and Gabriel met every night during the period of Ramadan, the most sacred month of the Islamic calendar.

THE QUR'AN

Generosity was one of the many qualities of Prophet Muhammad, who is believed by Muslims to be a messenger and prophet of God. It is said by many that he was known to be the most generous during Ramadan. He is quoted by many as saying, "The believer is not the one who eats when his neighbor beside him is hungry. The believer is simple and generous, but the wicked person is deceitful and ignoble."

Followers of Islam believe that there are different levels of generosity. When we are acknowledged for giving, that is the most basic level, where there is an exchange and then notoriety for your gift. Giving anonymously is a higher level. The highest level is secret charity, when the recipient doesn't even realize he has received a gift. An example is leaving money someplace so that someone will find it.

The Five Pillars of Islam are the *shahada* (the Islamic creed professes that there is only one God, Allah, and that Muhammad is God's messenger), *salat* (daily prayers), *zakat* (almsgiving, charity, generosity), *sawm* (fasting during the sacred month of

Ramadan), and *hajj* (the pilgrimage to Mecca at least once in a lifetime).

Obligatory acts of charity, *zakat* in Arabic, purify the heart. Prophet Muhammad said, "The most generous is he who fulfills that which Allah has deemed obligatory upon him." Muslims would then deserve to be rewarded. But if they did not fulfill the zakat, they would be sinners and deserve punishment in this world, as well as in the hereafter.

The standard annual amount acceptable for *zakat* is 2.5 percent of net worth (assets – liabilities x 2.5 percent). That's *net worth*, not annual earnings. In modern times, Muslims are more concerned about paying *khoms*, or giving charitable gifts, the recipients of which are based on the private decision of the giver.

> Obligatory acts of charity, *zakat* in Arabic, purify the heart. Prophet Muhammad said, "The most generous is he who fulfills that which Allah has deemed obligatory upon him."

The Qur'an states: "And whatever you spend in good, it will be repaid to you in full, and you shall not be wronged" (Qur'an 2:272).

A Pew Research Center survey of more than 38,000 Muslims in thirty-nine countries found that 77 percent said they donated to charity.

CHAPTER THIRTEEN

BUDDHISM: 1.5 MILLION IN THE UNITED STATES (376 MILLION WORLDWIDE)

Riches ruin the foolish, but not those in quest of the Beyond. Through craving for riches the ignorant man ruins himself as he does others.

—DHAMMAPADA 355

Anthropologist and physician Dr. Paul Farmer has an impressive educational pedigree and a list of professional achievements that few can claim. Yet he didn't choose to use either for personal gain. Instead, the Buddhist generously has devoted his life to others in a valiant attempt to provide first-world health care to third-world people.

Farmer was born in Massachusetts and grew up as one of six children in a poor household in Florida. The family constantly moved from place to place, even from bus to boat. However, Farmer graduated as valedictorian of his high school class and won a full scholarship to Duke University. At Duke he came into contact with Haitian migrant workers, whose wretched living conditions planted a seed.

Upon graduating from Duke University in 1983, Farmer flew to Haiti, and he continued to visit while he attended Harvard Medical School. He founded the Zanmi Lastane clinic in Haiti in 1984. Zanmi Lastane's medical results were stunning. The clinic reduced the rate of HIV transmission from mothers to babies to 4 percent and developed remarkable methods for treating tuberculosis, the biggest killer of Haitian adults.

Farmer cofounded Partners In Health (PIH) while still a student at Harvard Medical School. PIH, a nonprofit organization that provides free health care and advocacy for the less fortunate, has established clinics similar to Zanmi Lastane in Peru, Siberia, and Rwanda. Dr. Farmer continues to advocate for equal health rights by challenging world health organizations' treatment of infectious diseases, which won him a 2009 Nobel Peace Prize nomination.

Farmer views all people worthy of care and concern and has been dubbed "the man who could cure the world" by author Tracy Kidder in his Pulitzer-prize-winning book about Farmer *Mountains Beyond Mountains*. In the book, Kidder explains that Farmer lived in a small peasant's house, slept only four hours a night, kept nothing for himself, donated his physician's salary to his clinic, and walked miles to take medicine to sick patients.

Says Kidder, "I was drawn to the man himself. He worked extraordinary hours. In fact, I don't think he sleeps more than an hour or two most nights. Here was a person who seemed to be practicing more than he preached, who seemed to be living, as nearly as any human being can, without hypocrisy. He is a challenging person, the kind of person whose example can irritate you by making you feel you've never done anything as important, and yet, in his presence, those kinds of feelings tend to vanish. In the past, when I'd imagined a person with credentials like his, I'd imagined someone dour and self-righteous, but he is very friendly and irreverent, and quite funny."

Farmer, who holds so many humanitarian awards and professional designations we cannot list them here, does not seek those things. Rather, he has established medical clinics in some of the most impoverished and dangerous places on earth including Kigali, Rwanda, where he lives with his wife and three children.

Seekers of Inner Enlightenment

The foundation of a Buddhist's path to enlightenment is generosity, which Buddhists believe releases people from their attachments and thus results in the beginning of spiritual awakening. Dr. Paul Farmer must be well on his way on his path to enlightenment; it seems that he has never been held back by attachments.

Buddhism is based on the teachings of Gautama Siddhartha (563–483 BC), thought by many in the Asian culture to be the most spiritually awakened person to have ever walked the earth. Thus, his followers, seekers of inner enlightenment, called him Buddha, or Enlightened One. The words in the quote at the beginning of this section are his.

THE TIAN TAN BUDDAH IN HONG KONG

According to M. J. Ryan, author of *The Giving Heart: Unlocking the Transformative Power of Generosity in Your Life*, Buddhists consider generosity to be the opposite of delusion.

The first training that the Buddha gave was always to practice generosity. He said it was the most basic way to experience freedom, because inner calm and happiness are fertilized by generous acts. This is why true generosity results in a feeling of inner joy. Not letting go creates inner turmoil. Thus, Buddha said that a true spiritual life is not possible without a generous heart.

The highest form of generosity in Buddhist teaching is giving wisdom in words and actions. There are also offering respect, giving your full attention to those you're with, or performing some simple act of kindness. Next is giving a material gift.

Buddhists believe that giving is mutual, so a person also has to be open to receiving. The recipient is to share his heart with the giver.

> Giving must be done with serene joy, and it results in merit but not when it is done just to attain merit. Giving generously implements the Law of Attraction. It's not that we give to be loved. It's just the law of the universe; as we give, we receive.

Generosity is one of the Ten Perfections of Buddhism. In Buddhism, generosity is seen as the antidote to greed, which is an unwholesome mental state that hinders spiritual progress. The belief is that when we give joyfully, our confidence increases, and we see that we don't need to be held back by things, which have no real value.

Buddhists strive to reach Nirvana, to eliminate all desires or cravings. They are taught that giving must be done with serene joy, which results in merit, but not when it is done just to attain merit. Giving generously implements the Law of Attraction. It's not that we give to be loved, but that as we give, we receive. It is also thought that when we give, we align ourselves with values like compassion, love, and joy.

Buddhists believe that those who don't practice generosity will be reborn in poverty; what a person gives away, he keeps; what he keeps, he will lose; without practicing generosity, one cannot build wealth; wealth left in the house can be stolen; without practicing generosity, one cannot achieve Nirvana; the tendency toward greed must be reversed deliberately, and those who do practice generosity with pure motivation, without attachment or expectation, will be rewarded.

CHAPTER FOURTEEN

HINDUISM: 1 MILLION IN THE UNITED STATES (850 MILLION WORLDWIDE)

Running after that cur, money, I have forgotten you, O Lord.
What a shame! I have time only for making money, not for you.
How long can a dog who loves rotten meat, relish the nectar?

—Basavanna, Vacana 313

In June 2010, a group of Hindus gathered to discuss radical generosity. They shared stories and ended up launching several projects as a result.

Following the event, one of their group, a Hindu woman named Charu*, reported seeing a television story on Christmas day about a person who distributed clothes to people in her community to keep them warm during the winter.

Charu was so moved by the report that she immediately set out to do the same in her community. That first day, she ended up knocking on almost three hundred doors, asking neighborhood residents if they would like to give clothes, shoes, or other items that would help those in need get through the winter.

She said that although some were unwilling to give, many opened their hearts and homes to her concern for those without needed clothing. Most of the neighbors even volunteered to deliver their possessions to her home.

When she returned home, Charu was overwhelmed by what she saw. Her living room was full of "clothes that could adorn

129

the most privileged," as well as shoes and blankets. And she received even more donations during the next few days.

One young woman who stopped by apologized for not having anything old to give. Instead, she had brought ten pairs of new shoes that she bought just to give away.

When Charu passed out clothes, instead of just handing each person a pair of shoes, she knelt down in a servant's posture, placing shoes on each person's feet in order to make sure that they fit.

Much to her surprise, this didn't turn out to be a one-time event. The rooms of her home continue to overflow with gifts. Now, with the help of many volunteers, she continues to distribute clothes, shoes, and blankets to those who would otherwise be in need.

*Name has been changed

The Generous Hindu

Charu's compassion for others resulted in generosity that not only supplied needed clothes to the poor but also gave others in her community the opportunity to give (which is another gift in itself). Generosity is one of the key Hindu components of daily morality, which include compassion, self-control, purity, fortitude, nonviolence, friendship, and truthfulness.

Hinduism originated in India sometime between 1800 and 1000 BC. It has no named founders. Hindus believe that there are many gods, but they choose to worship one.

Hinduism, also known as Santana Dharma, is considered to be more a way of life than a formal religion. It is based on the teachings of ancient scriptures, heard (*sruti*) and memorized (*smriti*). Sruti writings are about ancient Hindu saints who led solitary lives in the woods, which enabled them to develop a consciousness of the truths of the universe. Smriti writings are on memorized epics and universal truths.

Generosity, compassion, self-control, purity, fortitude, nonviolence, friendship, and truthfulness are key components of Hindu daily morality.

MAHATMA GANDHI, A LEADER IN INDIA'S STRUGGLE FOR INDEPENDENCE
OLGA POPOVA / SHUTTERSTOCK.COM

Hindus believe that there are three gates to hell, including *kama* (intense craving), *krodha* (anger), and *lobha* (miserliness).

Dana is the Hindu term for giving. Giving in Hinduism not only improves the quality of life in eternity, it also enhances the giver's current societal standing. *Dana* is such an important part of Hinduism that the word is a component of *dharma* (right conduct), *puja* (ritual), and *yjna* (worship).

CHAPTER FIFTEEN

UNITARIAN/UNIVERSALIST: 888,000 IN THE UNITED STATES (900,000 WORLDWIDE)

*You came into the world with fists closed and you
go away with open palms. So even while living
stretch your hand open and give liberally.*

—KABIR (CA. 1398–1470)

The First Parish Church of Concord, Massachusetts, and the Unitarian Church in Székelykeresztúr, Romania, have a deeply meaningful partnership. With origins in an ethnically Hungarian region of Romania that stretch back to the thirteenth century, this church has kept its spirit alive through the centuries, through communism, fascism, famine, and war.

When the tyrannical and murderous Romanian Ceausescu regime fell in December 1989, the smoke had barely cleared when Unitarian Reverand Gary Smith from the Concord church joined a delegation traveling to Transylvania. A partnership between his church and a the local Keresztúr Church began soon after, based on their "shared principles, a belief in freedom of conscience, the use of reason in matters of faith, and a tolerance of those with differing opinions."

Although never a partnership based on charity, financial aid became vital in helping the Keresztúr ministry to rebuild and carry out its countless responsibilities. With financial help from the Concord church, the crumbling Transylvanian house of worship was repaired and rebuilt as necessary. The Concord church even sent its youth groups to provide free physical labor to help get the job done. Meanwhile, sponsorship of Transylvanian students became a priority as well, with the church in Concord helping to provide133 students with essential educational support.

Through the years the churches exchanged visits, attended weddings and graduations, and celebrated births with their adopted sister congregations. Nearly a generation of worshipers had grown since the relationship began. Over the years, the well-used church facility in Concord became due for its own renovation.

The usual enthusiastic American-style efforts at fundraising began. But unbeknown to the parish church, the Keresztúr Unitarian community—made up of many who live on meager incomes or subsistence level pensions—began an effort as well. The result of this undertaking was announced in the following letter. It is the evidence of the circular energy and generosity of love.

Dear Brothers and Sisters from Concord!

We love you all and try to express this love whenever we meet or think of you. We have learnt from the Bible, and life has taught us, that: "A friend is a loving companion at all times and a brother is born to share troubles" (Proverbs 17:17).

You are now repairing and enlarging your church. In these hard economic times, this isn't an easy undertaking. Therefore we would like to give something back after all the help you have given to us, year by year. I suggested to our leading board that we organize fundraising in order to help on your project. My suggestion was greeted with joy, and people asked with tears in their eyes, can we do this?

Yes, we can. The proof is that a retired person from our board was the first to offer $100. This is half his monthly pension. A businessman also offered $100. Then a student who was once sponsored by your student scholarship program offered $100. And at the time our gift was only a rumor. We made it official on our Thanksgiving Day ...

The leading board of our community has determined that by the end of October, $10,500 will be collected and sent to you. Please take our offer with love. God bless your work and lives.

With love,
József and the Congregation of Székelykeresztúr

Sacrificial Generosity

At first blush, one might think this is just a story about two groups helping each other. But consider that while it is possible that the gifts given by the people from Concord were given from excess, since a family in the United States makes ten times as much as a family in Romania, it's obvious that the gifts made by the congregation of Székelykeresztúr were given sacrificially.

Search for Spiritual Truth

The Unitarian Universalist Association was formed in 1961 from a combination of the American Unitarian Association (est. 1825) and the Universalist Church of America (est. 1866). Unitarian Universalism is a theologically liberal religion that is composed of people from various other religious and nonreligious groups. Its basis is the "free and responsible search for truth and meaning."

Rather than being unified by a creed, members share the understanding that each person's theology is based on his or her search for spiritual truth. Since their individual theologies are influenced by their former religious associations, Unitarian Universalists have a wide range of beliefs.

Unitarian Universalists believe in God. They believe that we should be generous with each other as a response to God's generous gift of the world, and that giving enables them to remove themselves as their perceived center of the universe. It is believed that releasing our hold on material things leaves us with palms open and our minds no longer fixated on material possessions, which spurs further giving, all resulting in joy.

CHAPTER SIXTEEN

WICCAN/PAGAN/DRUID: 433,000 IN THE UNITED STATES (NO WORLDWIDE ESTIMATE)

Bide within the Law you must, in perfect Love and perfect Trust.
Live you must and let to live, fairly take and fairly give.

—THE WICCAN REDE

Her neighbor is elderly, so Linda and her sons often help her carry things, sweep her driveway, mow her grass, and do other errands for her. Of course, they don't expect an elderly woman to reciprocate by coming over and helping with their yard work. In fact, they don't want anything in return for their generosity. "We just do a little of hers when we do ours, because it's the right thing to do," says Linda.*

This neighbor, she says, bakes the most awful oatmeal cookies known to mankind. But when she comes to the door offering Linda's family a plate full of them in thanks for mowing her grass, they gratefully accept them, even though they know she lives on a fixed income and probably can't afford to give away food. And even though they always end up feeding her cookies to the chickens, they have no intention of short-circuiting the Prosperity Cycle.

As Linda's Pagan clan taught her, in the Prosperity Cycle things are cyclical. They believe, as Linda says, "It's like an electrical current. You can turn it on or off, but nobody wants it turned off. That's bad for everybody."

She explained, "In order to keep the Prosperity Cycle going, our neighbor did not need to be generous back to us. There is really no need for reciprocity. But if we hadn't accepted the cookies gratefully, we would have not only stifled our own cycle of generosity and prosperity, but by not allowing her to give, we would also have stifled hers, and that is not a nice thing to do to someone.

"We're Pagans from the 'white' path, the path of positive energy. We try to put as much positive energy and feelings out into the world as possible."

Linda and her family give as much as they can without jeopardizing their own health, safety, and welfare or that of their family members. They don't concern themselves with concepts like giving a percentage to a church. They just give as much money, food, and energy as they can without harming their own family.

"We believe that by following the principles of the Prosperity Cycle, we have resources to spare, because energy flows out and back again, bringing blessings along with it," Linda explains.

The concept of paying it forward, made popular in the movies a few years ago, is a tenet that Linda and her family live by. "I gave a boy at the corner store some change this morning, because he was short of money for his school snack," she said with a smile. As she always has, she helps others whenever she can and happily accepts help from those around her. It's a Pagan way of life.

*Linda requested that her last name not be used, because recognition for generosity has no place in her belief system.

Origins

Druidism traces back several thousand years from the end of the prehistoric Ice Age. To symbolize a spiritual rebirth, as well as that of creative expression, Druids were taken into the belly of Mother Earth, into caves and man-made mounds, where their senses were deprived and from which they would be reborn, their creative genius released into the light of day.

Pagan religious movements have their origins in the

Greco-Roman world, rather than the Middle Eastern Abrahamic religions.

Wiccan is a nature-based belief system that was inspired by Margaret Murray (1862–1963) and organized by Gerald Gardner (1884–1964) from the 1930s to 1950s. The natural world is seen as part of the divine. It is based on ancient religions of prehistoric Europe. To Wiccans, the God and Goddess, male and female, are separate but equal deities, and they believe that people, the natural world, and the deities are inseparable.

THE PENTAGRAM IS A FIVE-POINTED STAR THAT IS USED AS A SYMBOL OF WICCA BY MANY ADHERENTS.

Under the banner of Modern Paganism, Wicca and Druidism are often grouped together, because they have more in common than separating them (nature worship, gods and goddesses, religious freedom, positive ethics, magic, and reincarnation).

Wiccans are not devil worshipers but people who practice life-affirming, nature-oriented religion.

Druid ethical guidelines are based on several Celtic virtues, including generosity (hospitality and generosity of spirit by giving others latitude to be who they are), strength (courage, physical strength, and strength of heart to do the right thing) and truth (honor, loyalty, and justice).

Pagans/Wiccans believe in the Cycle of Prosperity. They believe that prosperity flows like electricity, that the circuit must be complete to keep it moving, and that it can be turned off instantly, like flipping a switch.

A key component of prosperity is generosity, which can be expressed with money or good deeds. But that generosity must be sent out with no expectation of receiving anything in return.

To keep prosperity flowing, the intended recipient needs to be open to receiving, and that goes both ways. In other words, if you are serving somebody who then offers a gesture of generosity to you and you resist, because, let's say you don't believe the person can afford to give to you ... you just flipped the switch, and the flow of generosity (like electricity) is cut off.

In the Cycle of Prosperity, just because you give doesn't mean that you will receive. When you send out positive energy, you will receive blessings, not necessarily riches, in return. Pagans/Wiccans stress maintaining a positive outlook, being generous, and looking for the best in everything. They believe that what you send out will determine what you get back.

> A key component of prosperity is generosity, which can be expressed with money or good deeds. But that generosity must be sent out with no expectation of receiving anything in return.

The ancient Pagan deity Befana was a gift-giving Roman goddess. If you are generous but are not receiving blessings in your life, Pagan/Wiccans believe that you need to let the goddess know through ritual what you need.

The Holly King was a Celtic winter god. Thor and Tomte were Norse gods who rode across the sky in chariots drawn by goats and gave presents to children at the end of the year. All of these have fed into the legend of the man who epitomizes generosity by showering all of the children of the world with gifts, Santa Claus.

CHAPTER SEVENTEEN

SPIRITUALIST: 164,000 IN THE UNITED STATES (NO WORLDWIDE ESTIMATE)

Avarice is unrestrained desire for wealth, and in its selfishness is utterly debasing. To gain wealth that it may be employed in works of benevolence, charity or culture, is as noble, as hoarding is ignoble.

—HUDSON TUTTLE, *THE ETHICS OF SPIRITUALISM, SYSTEM OF MORAL PHILOSOPHY FOUNDED ON EVOLUTION AND THE CONTINUITY OF MAN'S EXISTENCE BEYOND THE GRAVE*, 1878

In 2005 Anita Teig gave birth to a baby girl. Like all babies, when she was hungry, she cried. It was a deeply unsettling cry that Anita had heard before, a cry that demanded a reaction, a cry that resonated as a memory from her childhood, when she heard the sounds of desperate children for whom there was never enough food.

Born in India, Anita was used to hearing the cry of hunger, and as any new mother knows, there is something in a baby's cry that raises an alarm. For Anita and her husband, Al, living in Massachusetts, the cry was a call to help. And not just by making sure their little one got the food she needed, but by returning to India to do what they could for the countless children who lived under the shadow of hunger every day.

To answer this need, the couple decided to identify families with babies in need and to personally pay for nutrition through those first, most critical months of life. For about $400 a month, they figured, they would be able to feed fifty-five infants each month. Through a network of family and friends in Chennai,

India, they located infants and their mothers who needed help and established logistics for identification and distribution.

But India is a big country, the poverty overwhelming.

The first distribution in March 2006 was a huge success. Families who enrolled in the program came each month to Anita's family house in India, where her father and her brother and sister-in-law handed out bags with formula and one article of clothing or a toy to each mother who arrived with her baby.

But as the days went by, more and more families began arriving and pleading for assistance. It became clear to Anita and Al that they would have to do more. And so, with the help of extended family members in the USA and India, they collected donations to support more infants in their developing years: Babies Need Food was born.

Carole Lynne, Al's mother and a Spiritualist minister, joined them to distribute food in India—an experience that she says "changed her life forever." She learned that many of the mothers had walked three miles in the hot sun in order to get to the food for their babies—and would walk back another three miles with their children on their backs or in their arms. She began to personally connect with them and to understand the desperation in these women's lives, and she made a commitment to herself and Spirit to support them.

Back in the United States, Carole Lynne started talking about Babies Need Food to her students and to people at the Spiritualist churches that she serves. She told them that each time she was able to raise between $150 and $200, a baby could be enrolled in the program and receive formula until age two. And if necessary, this child would also be seen by a pediatrician.

Largely through her efforts, two Massachusetts churches— Greater Boston Church of Spiritualism and the First Spiritualist Church of Salem—took part in fundraisers for Babies Need Food. When Carole Lynne went to California, the Golden Gate Spiritualist Church and the Central Spiritualist Church in Sacramento also raised money. Over the past eight years, Spiritualists have raised thousands of dollars to feed hungry babies in India.

Babies Need Food has become, to Carole Lynne, a family effort that is certainly a labor of love. And the larger family of Spiritualists from across the country has supported this effort and made it possible for Anita and Al to feed an ever-growing number of babies from poor families for whom hunger would otherwise be an unremitting shadow.

The Law of Love and Generosity

The Law of Love, found in Natural Law Governs, a Study Book on Spiritualism, illustrates how Spiritualists perceive love and generosity:

"The law of love is the creative source and power of all life. The realization of this law is the highest goal to be attained; love is purifying. It is the power that lifts the heart and soul to the highest spiritual awareness. The highest levels of consciousness are achieved through this law. Living in the law of love provides one with freedom—freedom from negativity, jealously, hate, resentment, and revenge. This new found freedom leaves us free to pursue the positive goals of peace, harmony, happiness and contentment.

"By living this law we can create a new and positive awareness for, not only ourselves, but others as well. The love principle is the action of giving and its reaction of regiving; it is the constructive force of all forces and thus the highest vibration. The spectrum of love is patience, kindness, generosity, humility, courtesy, unselfishness, good temper, guilessness and sincerity."

Rapping on the Walls

Spiritualists say that sisters Katie and Margaretta Fox heard rapping on their walls one night in 1848. The rapping lasted, they say, on and off, for several days. Finally, on March 31, 1848, the girls' mother, Margaret, realized that each rap stood for a letter of the alphabet. Based on that code, the rapping spelled a name, Charles B. Rosna, and explained that he had been killed in their house. Human bones were later found buried in the cellar.

That was the birth of the modern American spiritualism movement.

To this day, spiritualists say that the rappings prove that a real live person in Spirit was talking to those left on earth. God had provided spiritualists, they say, with a very natural way of talking to those people they loved who had gone to Spirit.

Followers of Spiritualism believe that our consciousness survives physical death and that spirits of the dead want to and can communicate with the living. Spiritualists convene in groups with mediums, who conduct séances to connect them with the departed.

IT IS BELIEVED THAT PRESIDENT ABRAHAM
LINCOLN ATTENDED SÉANCES.

They believe that spirits are closer to God than living humans and that spirits are capable of growth and perfection.

Followers rely on spirits as guides, because they believe that

143

they are far more advanced than humans and are, therefore, a source of profound wisdom about moral and ethical issues.

> Followers rely on spirits as guides, because they believe that they are far more advanced than humans and are, therefore, a source of profound wisdom about moral and ethical issues.

Spiritualists believe that their Declaration of Principles was communicated to them from the Spirit world through a medium. The first six of the nine principles were adopted in Chicago in 1899. Although none mention generosity specifically, Number 6 is the Golden Rule: "Do onto others as you would have them do onto you." In the Spiritualist Lyceum (simplified) form this is restated as, "Be kind, do good, and others will do likewise."

Through their good works to support Babies Need Food in India, Spiritualist followers throughout the country are generously living the Golden Rule.

CHAPTER EIGHTEEN

NATIVE AMERICAN RELIGION: 145,000 IN THE UNITED STATES (NO WORLDWIDE ESTIMATE)

> See to it that whoever enters your house obtains something to eat, however little you may have. Such food will be a source of death to you if you withhold it.
>
> —NATIVE AMERICAN RELIGIONS. A WINNENBAGO FATHER'S PRECEPTS

Martin Brokenleg's father was the first Native American on the Sioux (Lakota) Rosebud Reservation to be ordained as an Episcopal priest, and his parishioners lived in one of the poorest counties in the entire United States. At the end of a visit to a tribe member's home, his father would pray, and after praying he would inconspicuously slip the gift of a large-denomination bill into the hand of the head of the household as they shook hands.

The Lakota language saying repeated most frequently is "*Mitakuye Oyasin,*" which means, "We are all relatives." The priest didn't flaunt his generosity, and those who received it weren't expected to make a fuss. After all, that's just what relatives do.

Martin Brokenleg, EdD, is now a professor of Native American studies at Augustana College, Sioux Falls, South Dakota, dean of the Black Hills Seminars on reclaiming youth, and coauthor of *Reclaiming Youth at Risk: Our Hope for the Future.*

At the time when South Africa's apartheid laws were being lifted, he was visiting that country to address one of the first interracial youth worker conferences held there. In attendance were several hundred youth professionals.

While discussing generosity, Martin explained that the Lakota say that one should be able to give away anything "without the heart pounding," which means, "without your pulse quickening." In the audience, voicing frequent critical comments, was a white woman who had made a point about showing her obvious discomfort with people of color—including Martin—at the podium. From her seat, she attempted derision. "I really like your earrings!" she boomed.

It is a tradition in Lakota society to pierce the ears of a child to symbolize that the ears are open to spiritual teaching. The Lakota earrings he was wearing had been given to Martin by his parents as he was leaving to travel to a country that had a reputation for abusing people of color. Following his peoples' custom, he calmly walked to the woman, removed the earrings, and gave them to her.

Obviously embarrassed, she repeated Martin's earlier words, "Oh, now *my* heart is pounding." He replied, "It is just joy."

Later, another white woman approached Martin as he left the building. With tears in her eyes she said, "I saw that you gave your earrings away." She opened her hand, showing him her earrings, and said, "These were my mother's, and she wore them the last two years she was alive. They are very precious and have been handed down from relative to relative." Then she put them into Martin's hand.

"I still have them in a little box on my dresser so I can be reminded of her generosity. Perhaps some day I will find the right occasion to give them away," Martin said.

Lokota Generosity

It is obviously no coincidence that Martin and his father were so generous. The value of generosity is deeply rooted in their religion.

Wacantognaka

The English word generosity derives from the Latin word generōsus, which means "of noble birth," which itself was passed down through the Old French word genereux. Long before Europeans arrived on our shores with their traditions, Native

American religion taught its followers to be generous with one another. They believe that the reason to become prosperous is not to hoard riches but to be in a position to help others.

Wacantognaka, the Lakota word for generosity, means to contribute to the well-being of one's people and all life by sharing and giving freely.

Although many white settlers believed that Native Americans had no religion, the opposite was true.

Native Americans were highly spiritual, and tribal communities had various spiritual beliefs. They believed in what some tribes called Wakan Tanka, the great spirit. Young men of many tribes would engage in a coming-of-age ceremony that celebrated their connection to a great spirit. An example of these practices might be that the young man would fast and go into a trance until he saw an animal that became his spirit friend. They believed that there were living souls in the trees, stones, and stars. When they came across a beautiful scene, they would stop and worship.

SITTING BULL IN 1885

Sitting Bull, whose given name was Tatanka-Iyotanka

(1831–1890), was a Lakota. He lived to exemplify the tribe's four cardinal virtues, which were bravery, fortitude, wisdom, and generosity. He was known for being humble, kind, and generous. He always gave meat to the needy—even to hungry dogs. He gave buffalo that he had killed to hunters who weren't as fortunate as he. Prestige, in his tribe, was earned by giving away property, not by accumulating it.

After he surrendered to the US government, Sitting Bull went on the Wild West Show tour of the country with Buffalo Bill Cody. Annie Oakley, who was also in the show and became a close friend of Sitting Bull, said that he gave most of the small amount he earned from the show to poor children he met wherever they performed.

ANNIE OAKLEY

Crazy Horse, also a Lakota, was similarly generous. In fact, when hunts produced little and his people were hungry, he would not eat.

The homes of Iroquois were always open, to strangers as well as to each other. They were known for giving up their food, their beds, and their clothing when others were in need. No sacrifice was too great.

Sitting Bull was known for being humble, kind, and generous. He always gave meat to the needy, even to hungry dogs. He gave buffalo that he had killed to hunters who weren't as fortunate as he was. Prestige, in his tribe, was earned by giving away property, not by accumulating it.

When the white man defeated Native Americans and drove them on to reservations, most whites assumed that the Indian culture would perish. But John Fire Lame Deer (1903–1976), a Mineconju-Lakota Sioux, recounted story after story of Native American businessmen giving up all they had accumulated to care for the less fortunate, not just members of their own family but anyone from their tribe.

He told of an Indian industrial worker who lost a leg in an accident and spent his entire insurance settlement of $15,000 to put on a two-week feast for his entire family. When it was over, he said he wished he could lose his other leg so that he could do it again.

To explain the differences between the Native American and white cultures, Lame Deer said, "Indians chase the vision, white men chase the dollar. We are lousy raw material from which to form a capitalist. We could do it easily, but then we would stop being Indians. We would just be ordinary citizens with a slightly darker skin. That's a high price to pay, my friend, too high."

The Huron were known for giving feasts. There are endless stories of extreme generosity being commonplace among the Omahas, the Cheyenne, the Blackfoot, the Oglala Sioux, and other tribes.

The word generosity might have originated on the opposite side of the Atlantic Ocean, but the practice of living a generous life was deeply embedded in Native American culture long before Europeans ever set foot on American soil.

PART IV: HOW WORLD CHANGERS GIVE

There's no good reason to be the richest man in the cemetery.

—Colonel Sanders (1890–1980), founder of Kentucky Fried Chicken

The Dos and Don'ts of Giving

This is the "how to" section of the book. Here, you will find practical information that you can apply to start on your giving journey. Not all of these steps need to be used by everybody. How closely you follow them will depend upon your individual personality. However, we recommend that you read the next two chapters to determine if these time-honored principles can help you in your journey.

CHAPTER NINETEEN

GIVING LIKE A PRO: CHARITABLE TOOLS ENHANCE THE EXPERIENCE

Earn all you can, save all you can, and give all you can.

—ANDRE GIDE (1869–1951), FRENCH AUTHOR
AND NOBEL PRIZE WINNER FOR LITERATURE

George and Jennifer Reed* were wild about their pastor. When he kicked off the New Year with a highly motivating sermon on generosity, they left the church that Sunday on fire about committing more to improve their community and the world. Increasing their giving was all the couple could talk about during brunch after church.

Together they determined the total that they would give for the year and committed to attending more charitable events to learn about the good works being done in their local urban area. They decided to try to spread the wealth around a little more, to give the money they had earmarked for charity to as many local charities as they could.

The months went by; as the result of their attendance at charitable events and their response to mailers from organizations they had never even heard of, they found themselves overwhelmed with requests. Before they were halfway through the year, they realized that, at their current rate of giving, the amount they had budgeted would be gone very soon. Also, they realized that they hadn't received tax receipts for their donations from some of the organizations; they would have to remember to request them before filing their next tax return.

When Jennifer told a neighbor, who was also a member of

their church, that she and George weren't enjoying the giving experience like they had thought they would, the neighbor recommended that the couple have lunch with her financial advisor to see if he could help them find a better way to go forward. "We were feeling overdue for some direction," said George, so they made an appointment.

According to Jennifer, "It turned out to be some of the best advice we have ever received. The advisor suggested using a donor-advised fund, which he said would provide us a single tax receipt for the year, even if we gave to twenty charities. Tax time would be much more manageable. And we decided we would call it the Reed Charitable Fund—good name, don't you think?"

The advisor also helped them focus on what their true passions really were. For Jennifer, it was counseling unwed mothers, and George really wanted to help the poor. Their advisor recommended that before they gave the next dollar, they each visit local charities that worked in those areas. So George went down to a local homeless shelter, and Jennifer made an appointment to visit a pregnancy care center. After tours and brief discussions, they both found themselves signing up as volunteers.

George soon began to look forward to the evenings that he spent mentoring young homeless men, coaching them about the value of continuing their education, as well as how to dress for and handle job interviews. He says, "When I really got to know these men, it hit me like a ton of bricks—with a few bad decisions, it could be me sitting there."

Jennifer says, "George and I are unable to have children, so I do my best to emphasize to each girl what a truly special gift her baby is and how important it is that she work to provide a life of opportunity for the child ... I really only thought George and I would put some money into these causes, but what has made this really fulfilling is our personal connection to the people who need help. Who knew we could be mentors?"

Their new financial counselor also helped the couple integrate their giving with their total financial picture, including investments and tax planning, and introduced them to some giving tools that greatly simplified their charitable efforts.

"The beginning of our giving effort was absolute chaos, when we were just writing checks to a bunch of charities," says George, "but now our finances are in order, our records are organized, we're intensely focused on a few charities that we're highly involved with, and we are enjoying just that sense of engagement and the good feelings that other people always told us about."

*Names have been changed

How the Pros Do It

Giving sounds easy, but George and Jennifer learned the hard way that they didn't instinctively know how to do it.

If you wanted to golf like a pro, sing like a pro, dance like a pro, or do anything else like a professional, you would probably seek advice from those who had gone before you, including a seasoned coach to teach you how to do it right.

Giving like a pro is no different; to do it right, you need to find an experienced charitable professional to walk you through the process. These individuals serve givers through organizations that facilitate giving. To locate them, visit the Resources page of WorldChangingGenerosity.com. In addition to seeking a referral to a financial advisor, you should also find an experienced CPA and/or tax attorney. To help you be the best that you can be, you should learn all you can from your coach about the giving process, the traps to avoid and the tools that are available. That's giving like a pro!

Your Giving Journey

To begin on your giving journey:

1.   If you are religious, pray for wisdom and guidance.

2. Identify your values and priorities in life by considering seriously what your religion or belief system says about generosity (Part III: Generosity as a Value).
3. Determine what passion is in your heart (more about this in the next chapter).
4. Tap into the wisdom of those with experience.

For some busy people, due to time constraints, including heavy work and family schedules, the best way to be involved is to provide money to an effort. In many cases, that is the best way to help. If you want to fund the effort to cure ovarian cancer, for example, you probably won't be volunteering in the laboratory. What the researchers need is funding.

Clearly, most charities require monetary assistance to continue their work. But it is great if you become more deeply involved with at least one organization that you help to fund. You will find that sometimes the volunteer fit is perfect. Other times, you will end up making a move and getting involved somewhere else.

Choosing and sometimes changing where to invest your money and time are things that correctly fit into the generous life of one who practices benevolence.

We have friends who build wheelchair ramps. The group is made up of men who love to help someone and also love to get out on a Saturday morning and use power tools. They laugh and have a great time while they work. Others are behind-the-scenes people. They'd much rather do accounting work for a charity or offer multiple scenarios for potential solutions to the issues facing a fledgling organization. Find a volunteer opportunity that fits what you enjoy doing and the talents you have. To give your money, find an approach that works for you as well.

Giving Modes

We identify giving modes as reactive, impulsive, strategic, and spontaneous. Reactive giving isn't bad, unless that's all you do. Like many other impulsive responses, there could be a more effective approach. Of course, the strategic giver is the one who puts the most into understanding where his or her money is going and perhaps gets the most out of it. We are also big fans of the spontaneous giver. Giving in any form is a response of love to a serious need. Do plan, but the most important thing is to enjoy giving no matter how you do it.

Reactive

For many people who could be known as emerging givers, giving is initiated by social media, or perhaps a call made by a telephone solicitor on behalf of a charity is received. Reactive giving involves very little, if any, investigation, no proactive effort on the part of the giver, and doesn't usually provide an opportunity for the giver to have any direct involvement with the work being done by the charity or its impact. But large-scale tragedies, like the tsunami in the Pacific Rim, may be impetus for a reactive extra gift. Just make sure it goes to a reputable group that has a history of using such gifts wisely.

> We have friends who build wheelchair ramps. The group is made up of men who love to get out on a Saturday morning and use power tools. They laugh and have a great time while they work. Others are behind-the-scenes people. Find a volunteer opportunity that fits what you enjoy doing and the talents you have. To give your money, find an approach that works for you as well.

Impulsive

Many people give to different charities every year in an instinctive manner based mostly on impulse. Again, this approach doesn't usually enable the giver to become engaged with the charity. Experienced givers will tell you that, overall, it is wise to focus your giving primarily on your areas of interest. If a special event or fund is raising money outside of your interest area, a one-time gift might be in order. Just consider it in the overall picture of your giving plan.

Strategic

Strategic givers plan, and planning requires time and effort. Doing the soul-searching and research to make sure your gifts are doing the most good in an area you care about is the mark of an experienced giver. For some, this approach reflects a belief that people are stewards of resources, with an inherent duty to use funds wisely—an idea that will be developed more in the next chapter.

One serious young man in his twenties we know analyzes each charity he supports. He told us that one charity could train a few seeing-eye dogs for $10,000. But the charity he donates to mobilizes doctors who can operate on and restore sight to ten people for that same $10,000. He just does the math. It makes him crazy-happy to give away a third of his gross pay because he totals up in his head the number of the blind who can now see, the children who are inoculated, and the families that are restored because of the help they have received through his generosity.

These intentional givers prefer to make giving an experience, often one that they share with other members of their family or like-minded friends. You'll often find them volunteering at a local food bank, medical clinic, or homeless shelter or taking on a mission trip in another state, country, or continent. Such action places the giver on the front lines, where he or she can not only witness what a charity does but also how it's done, plus the impact their work has on those being served.

These are mostly middle-class folks with jobs and families, just like you and me. They just schedule their efforts in to fit the life they live, enhancing their own lives and the lives of those to whom they give.

Spontaneous

In addition to being proactive and planning most of their giving, generous givers often add another dimension by reacting to personal needs that they observe, regardless of the absence of any reciprocating tax benefit. For example, some people will pay the toll for a stranger behind them in line at a toll booth; another person, like Michael Simas, chooses to buy groceries for somebody who needs some help, and there are those, like Debbie and Pete, who—pretty much out of nowhere—bought a new car for the lady who prayed for them in the bakery or Officer Thomas, who, rather than arresting a single mother for theft, bought the food that her family desperately needed. Impulsive, yes. This is impulsive altruism—kindness at its best.

When you pass someone begging for money on a street corner or at an expressway exit, have you occasionally felt drawn to dig into your pocket to give the person $1, $5, $10, $20, or more? It feels good, but you might wonder, are they really unable to find work? Will they spend the money I give them wisely? Let us absolve you of your fears. Here's the number-one rule about these kinds of gifts: it cannot matter what they do with the money. You can't control the end result of every magnanimous move you make. It only matters what you do. Judge the situation the best you can and do what you feel you should do. Period.

Remember, all we can do is what we can do. You can't fix every situation, but if you do a good thing and it doesn't work out, that's just the way it goes sometimes. No one in charitable giving hits a home run every time, but with practice and a little investigation, you can easily bat well over three hundred.

Just know gifts given to individuals are not deductible. It's not that charitable gifts can't be given in cash. You can deduct up to $249 in cash gifts per year per charity, but only if given to a recognized 501(c)3. The guy on the corner? He doesn't qualify by Internal Revenue Service (IRS) standards. For amounts over $250 given to a legitimate charity, make sure that you get a receipt to receive your federal income tax deduction.

> Intentional givers prefer to make giving an experience. You'll often find them volunteering at a local food bank, medical clinic, or homeless shelter or taking on a mission trip in another state, country, or continent.

Professional Representation

Before you venture too far on your giving journey, it would be wise to consider securing the services of a qualified financial advisor. Maybe you don't think you need one, and that may be true. But remember the impact of the financial advisor's guidance on George and Jennifer. We know lots of people who started out when they were young with an advisor by their side; to the last person, they credit their investing and giving success to the guidance they received.

Financial advisors either charge a fee or earn a percentage of the funds they manage for you. There are various schools of thought regarding which is better, but that is a decision that only you can make once you have been armed with all the available information. Since this could be one of the most important relationships you are ever going to strike up, it is critical that you interview prospective financial advisors with the same level of care you would exercise when considering someone to serve as a potential caregiver for your child or parent. If your giving is motivated by your faith, you should definitely seek out an advisor who shares your values. He or she will make giving infinitely more fulfilling.

Your advisor can also help you to determine how much to give. Some people set aside a percentage of their income, sometimes a 10 percent tithe, reflecting their religious beliefs, while others decide to give away as much as they spend on themselves. Some spend only what they actually need (not want), and give the remainder to help others.

Know that any giving is a great start on an empowered, circular life that gives as it receives and enriches the lives of those involved. So know that whatever you decide, if it works for your family and enables you to join in the effort to help others, it is the right amount.

If you have significant assets—in excess of half a million dollars of net worth—a high-level salary to protect, or if you hope to accumulate assets in this range, you should also seek qualified legal and tax counsel.

Charitable Experts

Remember, to learn to give like a pro you need a coach; you need guidance from some somebody who knows how it's done.

Although charities have development (fundraising) departments full of people willing to help you, they come with an agenda. After all, their job is to raise money for their particular charity.

To tap into the expertise you'll need, you're better off to find a completely impartial charitable expert within an organization that isn't looking at you as a potential donor. You can find faith-oriented charitable foundations with all the giving tools that will be introduced later in this chapter. If you aren't looking for a faith connection, you can turn to local community foundations or to the charitable arm of some financial services firms. Check the Resources page of WorldChangingGenerosity.com for links to organizations that facilitate giving.

Charitable-Giving Tools

Of course you can write checks directly to the charities that you wish to support. However, as is true with approaching any worthy endeavor, there are often more effective ways to accomplish the task.

Use of the right charitable tool can help to stretch your giving dollars, greatly simplify the tax-filing process, keep your records perfectly organized, vastly expand your knowledge of giving opportunities, introduce you to a community of like-minded givers, and provide needed income during your life, with the remainder earmarked for charity.

Private Foundation, Supporting Organization, and Trusts

When it comes to charitable giving, you've probably heard people mention a private foundation, a charitable remainder trust (CRT), a charitable lead trust (CLT), and several derivations of those tools. You might also have heard about a supporting organization. However, unless you're considering putting $100,000 or more into a trust or $1 million or more into a foundation, these tools are probably not for you. In the event that you are considering giving away sums like these, you need to seek counsel from a highly experienced tax attorney and/or CPA, as well as a financial advisor.

THIS INTERNAL REVENUE SERVICE BUILDING HOUSES SOME OF
THE 89,000 EMPLOYEES OF THIS GOVERNMENT AGENCY.

Donor Advised Fund (DAF)

If you would like to streamline your giving by parking a single
contribution, or multiple contributions, into a fund, with one
receipt for IRS purposes related to the year in which you make
each deposit, as well as the convenience of what operates like an
electronic charitable checking account, then you should open a
Donor Advised Fund, or DAF. It can easily accommodate what
you may dub your Family Foundation. Through your DAF, you
can then direct grants to charities organized under Section
501(c)3 of the Internal Revenue Code. Your gifts can be made in
the same year as your contribution(s) or in subsequent years—a
real benefit if you are dealing with a large sum: maybe an annual
bonus, an inheritance, or the gain from selling a business.

While gifts made by Private Foundations are public information, many DAFs make it possible to give anonymously. Charitable contributions to DAF's also receive higher levels of federal tax deductions than those made to Private Foundations.

Since individual family foundations are highly regulated and costly to support, many companies and individuals use DAFs for making all their charitable contributions. For families, it becomes a special opportunity to bring children into the decision-making arena and enables them to understand the needs of those who have less than they have. You can even give them a vote as to how the family's charitable giving will be directed.

Giving Circles

A giving circle is a group of like-minded people who donate into a pooled DAF and decide together where to give the money. These groups usually form not only to support local organizations but also to get involved and increase their knowledge and awareness of needs, most often in their local community, by volunteering for the charities that they support. In our town, a group of women have organized to put $1,000 each into their giving circle every year. This group now has more than one hundred members, meaning they have a substantial amount to give away, and they also work together on the front lines of the charities they support. They are joined in a sisterhood of kindness and care for each other and the needy of our area. They believe that it is one of the most beautiful and fulfilling ways to give.

A giving circle might grow from a group of quilters, office friends, business leaders, school children, motorcycle enthusiasts, fraternity brothers or sorority sisters, relatives, church members, etc. Pretty much any type of group will work.

> Know that any giving is a great start to an empowered, circular life that gives as it receives and enriches the lives of those involved. So know that whatever you decide, if it works for

your family and enables you to join in the effort
to help others, it is the right amount.

Charitable Gift Annuity (CGA)

Charitable gift annuities, or CGAs, are a great way to benefit
yourself financially until your death and then leave the rest
to a charity of your choice. Of special note is the fact that in
a low-interest-rate environment, the yield for the holder of a
certificate of deposit, savings account, or a money market fund
is far smaller than the normal CGA yield. So if you want to receive
a tax deduction, receive a fatter income during your life, and
bequeath the money remaining after your death, you should ask
about a CGA. The older you are, the higher the payments that
you receive will be.

Asset-Based Giving, or Nonliquid Gifts

Are you aware that most of us give the most of what we have the
least of? Doesn't sound like it makes sense, does it? Well, 80
percent of the charitable donations in our country come from
the checkbook, which means they are in the form of cash. Yet,
10 percent or less of our holdings are in cash. The other 90-plus
percent of our assets are what are called nonliquid holdings.

These nonliquid assets can also be given as charitable
donations, and there's a good reason to use them. Simply put, by
donating a nonliquid asset instead of selling it and then donating
cash, money that would otherwise be paid in the form of capital
gains taxes can either result in more to give or more to put in
your pocket.

The most common form of nonliquid gift is appreciated
stock; i.e., shares from publicly traded companies that have
grown in value. The receiving charity will usually sell the shares
right away, converting them to cash as soon as possible. The
benefit is that the giver receives an income tax deduction based
on the current market value of the shares, which includes the
gain in value since they were purchased. But because they are

owned by a public charity when sold, there is no tax due on the gain. This is a great way to turn tax dollars into charitable-giving dollars.

> Eighty percent of the charitable donations in our country come from the checkbook, which means they are in the form of cash. Yet, 10 percent or less of our holdings are in cash. The other 90+ percent of our assets are what are called nonliquid holdings.

Many charities also accept real estate. Deductibility, based on market value and tax benefits, works in a similar manner for the giver, but it often takes significant time to liquidate property.

To ensure the deductibility of a more complex gift, like part of a closely held business (Subchapter S, LLC, Limited Partnership, C Corporation), make certain that you seek counsel from highly experienced legal, tax, and financial professionals, as well as highly qualified charitable giving experts who have considerable experience in this area.

Although gifts like these are a huge blessing to all parties involved, they can be an IRS nightmare for the giver if handled improperly. For example, should the donor accept, in writing, any offer to purchase an asset prior to proper documentation that the gift has been made to charity, the entire transaction could be disqualified for deductibility.

These gifts can produce significant federal income tax savings based on the market value of the business (substantiated by a valuation performed by an independent appraiser) and savings of all or a considerable share of capital gains tax and reduced estate tax. Check the WorldChangingGenerosity.com site for connections to those who can guide you through these types of charitable gifts.

Using Charitable Giving Tools

Although it is unlikely that you will need all these tools, you should develop a relationship with a charitable giving counselor at an organization that can facilitate charitable gifts. When the organization has a tool that fits your particular situation, it will be made available to you. Check the Resource page of WorldChangingGenerosity.com for information on the latest innovative web-based tools.

CHAPTER TWENTY

DEVELOPING STREET SMARTS: SPREAD DOLLARS FARTHER WITH CHARITABLE DUE DILIGENCE, LEVERAGE, AND MORE

The best thing to give to your enemy is forgiveness; to an opponent, tolerance; to a friend, your heart; to your child, a good example; to a father, deference; to your mother, conduct that will make her proud of you; to yourself, respect; to all men, charity.

—BENJAMIN FRANKLIN (1706–1790),
POLITICIAN, WRITER, SCIENTIST

Conner Morgan* had heard a version of this story dozens of times. Conner was a charitable giving counselor for a not-for-profit organization; Bruce and Charlotte Ellington* were in their late seventies. Bruce was saying, "We've probably got ten or fifteen years left to do something that might impact some lives. Our friends who are active in a charity or two are really enjoying it. I guess we have spent the last fifty years giving our money to just our church and Michigan State, where I went to school. Although they are good organizations, we know there is more out there, more we could do, and maybe we could really enjoy doing it."

Conner started asking questions about their interests; he learned that because both of them had survived growing up in the aftermath of the Great Depression and had witnessed the effects of poverty, they wanted to do what they could to help poor children have some advantages in life.

Charlotte was intrigued about what she heard was going on

in Africa to help children who had been orphaned because their parents were killed by either the AIDS virus or tribal warfare.

"Well," Conner said, "you would probably be shocked to learn how many children right here in our town don't have enough to eat or access to basic health services or a clean place to live." He shared a few stories about two local groups that served that particular niche and recommended that they visit. If they liked what they saw, they might volunteer.

"That kind of involvement will give you the perspective you need to see if you'd like to invest your charitable dollars in the work they do," he said. He added that after this local, hands-on experience, they would be in a better position to decide if they wanted to venture across the ocean to tackle this same crisis in Africa.

Bruce and Charlotte started out by attending the annual fundraising dinner of one of the charities, where they learned about the severity of the problems that homeless and hungry children were experiencing in their own home town, as well as the services provided to them through the organization hosting the event. Greatly impressed by the leadership of the organization and the strategies the group was pursuing, they signed up as volunteers.

Their first assignment was serving lunch to the children. That was all it took. Bruce and Charlotte saw themselves in these children, and they were hooked. They volunteered to tutor the children in the subjects of English and history three days a week, and they began providing financial support.

Fast-forward three years; the couple now volunteers daily. Bruce is a member of the board of directors, and their financial gifts to this organization have increased, along with the fulfillment and enjoyment they get out of their efforts.

The couple continues to support their church and give an annual gift to their college. They also help fund another local effort that runs a summer camp for inner-city kids, as well as one that works with African orphans. But their hearts are with the kids they tutor, the kids whose lives are changed by Bruce and Charlotte's care, guidance, and love. They are changing the futures of those children, one child at a time.

*Names have been changed

Getting Street Smart

World changers are street smart. They know how to identify their charitable passions; they know how to conduct due diligence; they know how to apply leverage; they know how to conduct in-person visits; they know how to get the most out of volunteering, and they know how to evaluate a giving opportunity as a charitable investment.

Through their hands-on experience, Bruce and Charlotte began developing their own street smarts. With the help of their charitable giving counselor, they learned what to look for in an organization, including

- strong leadership;
- good stewardship of financial resources;
- transparency;
- selection of excellent employees;
- a fully engaged board of directors;
- a clear mission and vision;
- a strategic plan;
- measurable outcomes; and
- an adequate cash reserve.

You can speed up the process of developing street smarts by applying the advice offered in this chapter.

Step One: Identify Your Passion

When considering where to give, you should first determine where your passions lie. They could be in any of these areas:

- poverty: food, health, shelter, other necessities
- aid: emergency support, rebuilding of infrastructure

- religion: church, expanding the influence of faith, ministry work
- justice: human-rights violations, slavery, persecution, human trafficking
- culture: art, history
- individual development: education, job training, character

SOME OF THE 590,000 ORPHANS IN SOMALIA
SADIK GULEC / SHUTTERSTOCK.COM

Let's start from the thirty-thousand-foot view and work our way down. For example, you care about children. More specifically, you are concerned about orphans without families. You care about feeding them, or you're concerned with their housing needs. You care about the quality of their education. You might be more focused on the needs of local orphans than those on the other side of the globe. You might decide to volunteer at a local orphanage to get experience until you can save up enough to take a mission trip to Kenya.

Perhaps you are shocked by the idea of sex slavery or slavery in general. There are human rights groups that specialize in freeing and rehabilitating such people here and around the world.

Before jumping into volunteering and/or giving, walk yourself (or each other, if you are a couple or family) through a process like this to figure out where your true philanthropic passion lies. Keep going until you are satisfied that you have zeroed in on your sweet spot.

Step Two: Conduct Research

Once you have drilled down on your passion, the next step is to search for charities that serve the niche you have selected. This can be accomplished with information collected through a web search or supported by referrals from friends and experienced givers or from charitable giving experts whom you respect.

The charity you select must be classified by the IRS as a public charity under Section 501(c)(3) of the Internal Revenue Code. Churches, some 501(c)(4) organizations, certain government entities, and operating foundations also qualify. Organized under US laws, they are accountable to federal and state authorities, and donations qualify for deductions on federal income tax returns. Some states also allow such deductions.

The charity should have filed a Form 990 (or 990 EZ for smaller charities), a charitable tax return, which will be posted for your examination on the charity's website or at CharityNavigator. org or GuideStar.org. If the charity that you're investigating is not listed on one of these sites (younger or smaller charities might not appear) and their website doesn't enable you to download a copy of their Form 990, you can request a copy. This is public information. If they resist making it available to you, that is a red flag that you should not ignore.

The level of insight you can gather from conducting an investigation on the Internet and through e-mail correspondence is limited. Telephone conversations can help you to dig deeper, but of course, especially in the case of a larger donation, the best way to understand if a charity is truly worthy of support—of your time, talent, or money—is to make an in-person visit.

Step Three: Make an In-Person Visit

If you are considering making a sizable (a truly relative term) donation to an organization, you should make an appointment with a high-level organizational official. Make sure it is clear what subjects you want to cover and how much time will be made available to you. Ask to have the most recent annual report sent to you so that you can review it prior to your visit.

FACE TO FACE, YOU CAN REALLY GET A GAUGE ON THE LEADERSHIP OF AN ORGANIZATION.

From the research you conducted on the Internet, via e-mail, on the telephone, and your review of the charity's annual report (if you're not numbers-oriented, you can run the annual report by somebody who is), make a list of questions to ask during your site visit.

Here are ten questions (and supporting questions) that strategic givers may want to have answered:

Note that this list was developed from surveying private foundations as well as individual givers who give in the range of $10,000 minimum gifts. You might not find it necessary to dig anywhere near this deeply. On the other hand, if you are highly *detail-oriented, you might find the following list of questions—to ask others and some to ask yourself—highly useful.*

1. Since you are a key leader here, what is your story?
   - What drives you to stick with this?
2. What is the mission or purpose of the charity (the need it is currently addressing) and its vision (the problem it is attempting to solve) for the future?
   - Are its programs aligned with its purpose/vision?
   - Does this purpose/vision interest me?
   - Does it fit with my giving goals?
3. What is your target population?
   - How many were served last year?
   - How many people are projected to be served this year?
   - How do current results compare to goals?
   - What is the charity's performance history?
   - What are their geographic boundaries?
4. Does the charity have the capacity necessary to accomplish its purpose?
   - What is the budget? (If you're not numbers-oriented, before making a significant contribution you may want to run the budget/projections and annual report by somebody who is.)
   - Do you have the necessary personnel?
   - Do you have people with the talents/skills necessary to serve their purpose?
   - Do you have the infrastructure necessary to support the staff?
5. Does the charity have a plan (a strategy)? If so:
   - Has the necessary organizational structure with operational support been considered?
   - Does the plan identify critical behaviors or practices necessary for success?

- ○ What does success look like?
- ○ Have desired outcomes been clearly identified?
- ○ Are there metrics to measure outcomes?
- ○ Can this charity (and my contribution) truly make a difference?

6. Is the charity duplicating services already being provided by other organizations? If so:
    - ○ Is there a good reason why this charity is functioning in the same giving arena as others?
    - ○ What differentiates your organization from the others?
    - ○ Is there any potential for collaboration and/or consolidation?

7. Does the charity have a governing board of directors? If so:
    - ○ Who are they?
    - ○ Is the majority of the board independent from the executive leadership?

8. Is the charity's operational leadership qualified?
    - ○ Are they experienced?
    - ○ Would I entrust investment dollars to these people if they were running a private enterprise?

9. What are the charity's greatest challenges?

10. If you could change anything, what would it be?

If charity leadership has no way of measuring outcomes, the chances are pretty good that they really don't know if what they are doing is truly making a difference. If they do measure outcomes, make sure that you understand their metrics and that you are in agreement with the level of impact that is acceptable to them.

Step Four: Volunteer

If you are sending money to a charity overseas—in Africa or a mission in India, for example—regular volunteering will likely be impossible. But if it is going toward a local concern or one that allows you to take a mission trip, do consider volunteering or making the trip to their mission field before you make a contribution. Not only should this experience help you to determine if the charity you are evaluating is worthy of support, but rolling up your sleeves and jumping in at some level also enables you to experience the work they do firsthand to ensure that its purpose truly aligns with your passion.

TRY VOLUNTEERING FOR AN ORGANIZATION THAT WORKS IN YOUR AREA OF PASSION.

By volunteering, you can connect to a new community of friends with whom you can share experiences and develop close personal relationships over time. Personal involvement can also help you to assess the quality of the organization's staffing and support infrastructure.

To be most effective, you should try to match your skills and experience with the needs of the charity by volunteering to work in an area that would utilize as thoroughly as possible the strengths that you bring to the table.

If you are sending money overseas, to a charity in Africa or a mission in India, for example, regular volunteering may be impossible, but if

> it is a local concern, or one that allows you to
> come in on a mission trip basis, do consider
> volunteering before you make a contribution.

Your service as an unpaid volunteer is an invaluable benefit to charitable organizations. In fact, if most charities had to pay for the services of those who volunteer, they could not survive financially. More than sixty-four million Americans volunteered in 2011. These volunteering efforts totaled more than 7.9 billion hours and had an estimated value of $171 billion.

In addition to the sheer value of your volunteer hours, you also have a chance to leverage your service into cash for your favorite charity. All you need to do is gather some colleagues from work or some other group (club, church, etc.), visit SuperServiceChallenge.com, sign up, serve the charity, and submit (through a smart phone app) an amateur video or picture presentation describing how your team and those you served were touched by your group's gift of time and talent. Also, explain how you intend to continue serving and how the charity would use any winnings. In 2015, around Super Bowl time, the Super Service Challenge people distributed $2.5 million in prize money in increments from $1,000 up to $25,000 per winning presentation. Three $25,000 prizewinners were invited to attend the Super Bowl. Before the game, one was selected as the grand prizewinner and received an additional $25,000.

Final Step: Give

Once you're at the point of making a financial contribution, there are still several important considerations.

Consider It an Investment

When you are ready to consider giving, think of your donation as a charitable *investment*. Ask yourself, "Should I *invest* in this leader and his or her management team?" If you decide to move forward, keep in touch, and hold the charity accountable for performance.

If you tend to be a highly relational person who usually selects people to work with based primarily on how much you like them, be careful. You should also consider doing what strategic givers do: make sure that the charity deserves your support because you have objectively evaluated it as an investment, and it passed your test.

Take a close look at the charity's financial condition. Again, if you are not numbers-oriented, have somebody who is financially savvy do this for you. Is there enough cash on hand to meet current needs? Is the charity's level of debt acceptable? Are sources of projected revenue realistic? Does the charity have a track record of controlling expenses? It is critical that givers understand that either the charities they support are financially viable or that givers will be responsible to pump life into them on an ongoing basis to ensure that their important work will be continued.

Up the Ante

Once you have supported a charity for some time, you might want to consider making it known that you're interested in moving from serving on the front lines as a volunteer to the boardroom. It is an honor to serve on a charitable board, but it is a serious commitment that may require more time than you envision and carries with it fiduciary responsibility, which can translate into legal liability. Before committing, make sure you understand what will be expected of you as a board member, including the time requirements, and make sure that liability insurance for officers and directors is in place. Board members are often asked to serve because they bring to the table either affluence (expected to offer increased financial support) or influence (reputation and connections attract other desirable financial supporters).

Seek Alignment

Again, if you want to work with those who share your world view, faith-oriented foundations can help you give to your church, assist you in finding ministries that work in certain geographic areas or in the specific areas of interest that you care about, and let you know what, if any, restrictions they might place on your grant requests. Some local community foundations provide similar services.

On the other hand, if you are unaffiliated with any religious group and want to make certain that none of your gifts are received by a religiously affiliated charity, there are foundations that can help you as well.

See WorldChangingGenerosity.com for links to organizations that facilitate charitable giving.

Watch Out for Scams

Natural disasters bring scammers impersonating charities out of the woodwork. Once you start giving, be especially careful when contacted by telephone solicitors asking for donations following such tragedies. They can be after your credit card or bank account information in an attempt to steal your identity. Remember, no charity needs your Social Security number in order for you to receive a tax deduction. Keep that number between you and state and federal tax authorities only.

Apply Leverage

Whether you have $10 or $10,000 to give, wouldn't you like to multiply the impact of your charitable gift? This is known as leveraging your giving, and it can be accomplished in several ways.

Look for opportunities for matching gifts. Many times a wealthy donor, a foundation, or an employer will offer a 50- or 100-percent match for gifts up to a certain limit. Another way to leverage your giving is to convert what would otherwise be tax dollars into giving dollars by donating appreciated assets (see last chapter regarding charitable gifts of appreciated shares of publically traded companies, real estate, closely held business interest, etc.).

Micro lending is another way to leverage your giving dollars, because your original investment never stops working. It is an opportunity to give people a chance to earn their own way—often creating industries for entire villages in underdeveloped countries—and automatically uses the money to pay it forward to the next person with a dream.

The way it works is that you go to a micro lending website, read about the people and the loans they need, and decide whom you want to help. The total amounts needed can be small amounts, from a hundred to a few hundred dollars. The great thing is that micro loans are paid back to the charity, which then lends the money out again to help others capitalize and grow their businesses. The repayment rate is much higher than that of a US bank, because a very high level of peer pressure not to default is placed on borrowers by other members of their villages or groups.

The enterprise might be a tailoring or alteration shop, a food stand, or a rug-weaving business. Whatever it is, the idea is to teach a person to fish instead of giving fish—a hand up rather than a handout. Some charities provide regular updates on how your entrepreneur is doing, which makes being involved twice the fun.

Remember

Identify your charitable passions. Learn how to conduct due diligence and how to hold effective in-person visits. Get the most out of volunteering. Evaluate giving opportunities as charitable investments and, whenever possible, leverage your giving dollars.

Be street smart when it comes to giving, and you can be a world changer.

FINAL THOUGHTS

Cultural differences should not separate us from each other, but rather cultural diversity brings a collective strength that can benefit all of humanity.

—ROBERT ALAN (AMERICAN WRITER, ARTIST, AND SOCIAL ACTIVIST, 1922–1978)

The major religious and nonreligious groups in our country and around the world encourage giving, consider attachment to wealth and possessions as a major obstacle to spiritual maturity or true development, and share a natural love for their fellow man that manifests itself in generosity.

It's time to set aside political, theological, ethnic, and other differences and focus on the one critically important objective upon which we agree: the mission of changing the world through generosity.

Try to focus on what you're really doing. Remember that it isn't a $20 bill that you're about to give away. It is enough rice to feed a starving family in Africa for a month. It isn't a quarter that you put in the bucket but what could be the final amount required to cure a disease. The church donation you make isn't $50 but the electric service that keeps the lights on at the church-run food pantry.

A LITTLE CAN DO SO MUCH FOR THOSE WHO NEED OUR HELP.

Even after reading this book, you might think, "I'm not ready. Money is tight. How can I make a difference?" Remember that money isn't the only thing you can give, but also remember that very few problems ever get solved for free.

> It's time to set aside political, theological, ethnic, and other differences and focus on the one critically important objective upon which we agree: the mission of changing the world through generosity.

All of the reasons to make charitable giving a part of your life are too numerous to list. But just in case you've forgotten, here are just a few:

1. You won't feel powerless about the problem anymore. You'll feel like you are working to make the world a better place, whether by providing clean water for people without access to it or tutoring a child to reduce illiteracy.
2. You'll develop a closeness with the group of people you are helping, as well as others who are working to help.
3. You will become a role model by the very act of generosity.
4. You will be happier. (It's just true.)

If everyone cares—even a little—and if everyone gives—to the extent that they can, and to the extent that they are happy to give—then we, together, really can change the world.

Are you ready?

—Jim and Nancy Cotterill

THE PREQUEL

The great thing is, if one can, to stop regarding all the unpleasant things as interruptions in one's "own" life or "real" life. The truth is, of course, that what one regards as interruptions are precisely one's life.

—C. S. Lewis (1898–1963), British scholar and novelist

Our journey of generosity began in earnest in 2001, about a month before the infamous 9/11 attacks on our country. When the World Trade Center was hit, we were in so much trouble of our own, the violence of it all almost didn't register. Here is our story and how we came to write this book.

A WRONG TURN TO
THE RIGHT PLACE

Jim

Nancy and I had just sold our interest in a small magazine publishing company that I had started eleven years before.

She didn't feel well, so we stayed in on Friday night, which is unusual for us, because on Friday nights for thirty-some years we've been going out for dinner and then usually to a movie with Nancy's two sisters, Linda and Sally, and their husbands, Steve and John. Nancy's temperature wouldn't go down, but she finally went to sleep.

On Saturday, things got progressively worse. She had a raging headache. When her temperature started inching up to 105 degrees, I called our friend, Sue, an accomplished emergency room physician, who told me to get Nancy to the hospital—right away. Following a short debate with Nancy, which I won (only because she was very weak), I took her to the hospital, where the doctor told me that her condition was so bad that had I kept her home for the entire weekend, she could have died. Instead, with the application of some mighty strong antibiotics, she was on the mend within a few days.

What a relief!

About a week later at six o'clock on Sunday morning, the phone on my bedside table rang, waking me out of a sound sleep. I grumbled groggily, "Who would be calling us now?"

"Hello?" I answered.

"Mr. Cotterill?"

"Yes."

"I am a sergeant at the Monroe County Sheriff's Department. I have your son, Ted, here with me ... He's okay, but he has been in an automobile accident. Since he's a minor, we have to take him to the hospital, where you can pick him up."

Alarmed and upset, I got directions; we threw some clothes on and headed down to Bloomington, a little more than an hour south of our home in Indianapolis, Indiana, to pick up our son.

We learned that Ted had fallen asleep at the wheel (because he had been up almost all night), crossed an oncoming lane of traffic in his old Jeep Cherokee, broke off a mailbox post, went down an embankment, bounced off a mini barn, sheared off a sign post, and slammed into a chunk of concrete. His Jeep ended up on its side, resting on the hood of a parked car—indicating that he was airborne at some point. The force of impact pushed this vehicle into several other cars in a used car lot. In all, five cars were totaled.

On the way to the junkyard to get his personal belongings out of the Jeep, Nancy and I were vociferously parenting (read, lecturing) Ted regarding his carelessness and poor judgment about driving when he was so tired. Then we saw the mangled body of his Cherokee, which we had purchased because we thought it would be indestructible. We surveyed the scene in stunned silence. The lecturing stopped.

It was demolished, grill to bumper—a crumpled piece of metal. Anyone would think that a fatality was involved, but Ted only had a small cut on his leg and a sore back. To us, he had clearly had some kind of divine protection, and we thanked God for keeping our son safe during the accident.

Boy, did we need a break! It was a good thing that our annual summer vacation was coming up soon. All we could think about was just relaxing, celebrating that Nancy and Ted were fine and that our other, Chris, and I were healthy.

So a few weeks before September 11, 2001, Nancy, Ted, Nancy's sister Sally, her husband John, their kids Emily and Tommy, three of the kids' friends, and I packed up our SUVs, put our bicycles on the racks, and headed, as they say, Up North.

After a full day of singing to oldies in the car, talking like we never have time to at home, and stopping only to eat and to fill our gas tanks, we arrived at the dock right on schedule. As we had done probably twenty times before, we took the bikes off the racks, unpacked the vehicles, and got on the ferry that would take us to an island for a week of biking, golf, and much-needed rest.

All we had time for that night was our traditional dinner together at the local watering hole, a short walk—during which we discussed how great it was to have weathered the storms of illness and accident in our family—and then off to sleep.

The next morning (island time—almost noon) we took off for a full day of golf on the course that we fantasized about the rest of the year. It was a long, long day of letting others play through, because our group was much bigger than it was supposed to be.

Then, after dinner, as it got dark, we adults went out to relax in the big old white wooden Adirondack chairs that are always lined up in front of the old hotel, facing the water. It was exactly what we needed.

Just then, my son Ted rode up on his bicycle and asked me to go for a bike ride. I was tired. I didn't really want to get up, but I thought, *How many more times is my sixteen year-old son going to want to spend time with his old dad?* So I went.

It was dark. I was just in front of Ted. I turned to the right and strained in an attempt to see the shoreline.

I blinked and opened my eyes. The lights were very bright. I suddenly realized I was in a hospital bed. *What in the world am I doing in a hospital? How did I get here?*

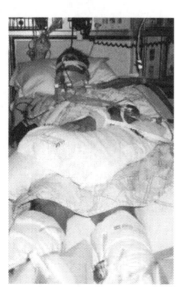

JIM AWAKENS, PARALYZED AND BREATHING ON A VENTILATOR

185

I immediately spotted a calendar on the wall about six feet from the foot of my bed. It was about two feet tall and three feet wide, and the days were X'd out with one of those thick black markers. According to that calendar, it was exactly one week to the day after Ted and I went for that nighttime bike ride. *What happened? Where's my family?*

I decided to get out of bed, but I couldn't move. I looked down at my arms and legs and thought, *Let's go!* They weren't tied down, but ... nothing. I tried to call out for some help, but I quickly realized that I had a pipe in my mouth, which was taped to my face; I couldn't talk. That's when I realized that not only was I paralyzed from the neck down, I was breathing on a ventilator.

Out of my peripheral vision I saw Nancy and her sister, Sally, walk into the room.

"You're awake!" Nancy said.

I nodded.

"Don't try to move," she said. "Just blink once for yes and twice for no. Do you remember what happened?"

I blinked twice.

Nancy

There was no room for me on the medical evacuation flight that took Jim to the hospital, so in the middle of the night, somebody called a pilot with a plane who said he'd take a charge card to get me to the hospital. I had been turned down by others who required cash, which I didn't have. It seemed like a godsend that we found a willing pilot—until we saw the plane. Ted, my sister Sally, and I got in this old, rusted, red single-engine plane with a pilot who looked like he'd just rolled out of a party after a long night.

The plane rattled so much I asked him if the door was really closed. He answered, "If it doesn't fly open, it's closed." He had an old rag with which he wiped off the condensation on the inside of the windshield so he could see; he often seemed confused about where he was headed. That's all I remember. Not landing, not getting to the hospital. I was exhausted, stunned, and yet hyperawake.

I do remember the waiting room. We waited, consulted

with doctors, and waited some more in a state of worry and confusion. A week went by, during which Jim tried his best to die. Twice, alarms went off, and nurses and doctors raced into his room with medical equipment to get him breathing again. It was starting to sink in: he wasn't moving. He couldn't move.

Every day, the doctors would ask me to come to a little room, no bigger than a cubicle, where they explained their latest prognosis. At first, they would tell me that they just didn't know what the long-term outlook would be. They were so busy keeping him breathing, they weren't as worried about whether he would walk again. But as the days went by, the meetings became full of warnings. They told me that I should be making arrangements for some kind of long-term care—that Jim would likely be a quadriplegic, a paraplegic at best.

Sally, my twin sister, who was there propping me up during the whole ordeal, would say, "Don't believe it. They don't know what they are talking about. He's going to get over this." The next day, they'd come up with something else, and she'd say it again, as if by popular demand Jim's spinal cord was going to jump back into action.

I remember one young doctor saying very casually to me, "Well, what does he do? If he's not a bricklayer and can get away without his arms and legs, he can still use his head." I think when he said that, my heart stopped. I couldn't talk. I just looked at him.

The same young doctor also was pushing me to let him operate, but our longtime friend (and noted neurosurgeon) Hank, with whom we were in constant contact back in Indianapolis, advised strongly against it. "Right now," he said, "an operation might only do more harm." So again, we waited.

Finally, Jim woke up. He had no memory of anything since getting on the bike. I let him know that he was in the intensive care unit of a trauma center 350 miles away from the island where the accident occurred. I told him that he and Ted had left the group to ride bikes down to the water and he had gone over a three-foot drop in the dark.

I explained he'd flipped over the handlebars and landed on rocks with the full weight of his body on the back of his neck. "It's broken," I told him. "We're just glad you're alive. A couple of times ... well, we didn't know if you'd make it. Anyway, Teddy started yelling for help. He thought you were dead. We all heard, of course. Immediately. We were only about forty yards away, and everyone took off running to get to you.

"You weren't breathing, so John started giving you mouth-to-mouth resuscitation, and I pumped on your chest. People were gathering around us, and you weren't responding. I know I was yelling at God to let you live, and our whole family was on their knees praying. Emily ran to find a doctor. Then some man literally appeared by your side and said that you were okay, and then it seemed like he just disappeared. But he was right. You started breathing on your own. By that time, the paramedics had arrived and started strapping you onto a board. They duct-taped your head and body flat and carried you away to the island clinic.

"You were in horrible pain. You were unconscious but kept crying out and moaning. Luckily, the doctor realized that you had a spinal cord injury and needed to get to a major medical center where you could get the care you needed. They called for an air transport jet and loaded you into an emergency van to get you to the airport.

"We know your spinal cord is damaged. We really don't know if the paralysis is permanent or not. The doctors told us they cannot tell. It just depends, they say. On what, I have no idea." I couldn't tell him the dire predictions they had told me.

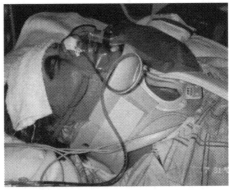

JIM WAS UNCONSCIOUS FOR A WEEK AFTER BEING AIRLIFTED TO THE TRAUMA CENTER.

Jim

Well, God, I thought, *since you obviously spared me, you must want me here for a reason. Please make it clear to me, because whatever it is, I'm all yours.* I was weak and in lots of pain, but I started praying, not only for healing but also that He would show me what I was supposed to do.

You know, they say that when a person is blind, their hearing is sharper than those who can see, or they notice a smell or vibration that signals a change in the room. That kind of thing.

I believe as I lay there, my senses were sharpened as well. I saw things more clearly. My life and my purpose seemed like a movie I could watch. What was once a future full of fuzzy ambitions, muddled by the grind of daily activity, became a clear path—a strong pull toward a certain goal.

Over the next few days in the intensive care unit of that trauma center, still paralyzed but now breathing on my own, I became acutely aware of the rapid movement of others in my room—doctors, nurses, orderlies rushing in and out, taking care of my every need because I could do nothing for myself.

I realized that life is about service. It was an epiphany for me; I'd always taken my abilities for granted. I'd thought I was pretty much bulletproof, the author of my own story—and now I was helpless. It was an unreal moment. Although I was paralyzed, with no assurance of ever regaining movement, I was imagining that God had a plan where I would be able to help others. Yes. Although none of it made sense, it all seemed possible. And for some reason, I wasn't afraid.

"So," I said to God (not out loud, but you get it), "unless you show me differently, I'm going to look for an opportunity to serve others." I started thinking that the writer John Piper was talking about me when he wrote, "It is better to lose your life than to waste it." *Well,* I thought, *I almost lost it. I'd better not waste it.* Soon after, I proved the doctors wrong. My left toes regained movement. Secretariat I was not, but that little movement gave me hope that I wasn't completely out of the race.

At the end of two weeks in the trauma center, Nancy,

who had been my constant protector during the whole ordeal, was flown with me in a medical jet back to Indianapolis. Now that the swelling in my spinal column had gone down and I—miraculously, according to doctors—had started to regain movement on my left side, I was sent to spend the next few weeks in intense physical rehab. Fortunately, I ended up in a world-class facility, Rehabilitation Hospital of Indiana. The folks there (to me, they're angels) got my legs moving, taught me to walk again, and showed me how to get along with just my left arm and hand, since my upper right side was still completely unresponsive.

Six months after intense, daily outpatient rehab following my weeks at RHI and a lot of prayer, functionality returned to my right arm and hand. At about that same time, after making my search for significance known to many others, I received a job offer to run a medical equipment company, which started me on the path of becoming a servant leader in my everyday work, serving people who used wheelchairs. It was an opportunity that was amazing in its timing and the effect it had on my life.

For five years, I got up every morning and prayed, "God, thank you that I can get out of bed, shower, dress myself, eat, drive (still using special equipment) to work, and serve others who aren't as blessed as I was to have recovered." And then I went to work every day, feeling great about serving the physically disabled.

But there was more I had to do. Have you ever experienced a time when you physically felt change coming? It's like the chair you're sitting in, which you used to love, just doesn't feel right anymore. Well, that's how I started to feel. I knew I had done all I could do at my job; I was being led to find a new challenge that would benefit the disadvantaged in our city.

At the same time, I knew that wouldn't be enough either. I also felt a strong pull to do something for those around the world who are without basic food, shelter, and health care. *Okay,* I thought, *those two things are diametrically opposed. Where am I going to find an opportunity that involves both?*

But just as healing had come and offers of work that filled my new criteria had landed out of nowhere on my desk, I happened to be talking to a friend about my new direction, and within weeks I took on the leadership for a local start-up Christian foundation.

When I met with one of the founders, he told me that through the foundation, donors would be able to support local charities and ministries that do the kind of work that can transform our community, or they could choose to support an orphanage in Ukraine or fight AIDS in Africa. In other words, they could help underprivileged people in our city and around the world. While it all sounded eerily like my dream come true, I innately knew that this was not merely a series of fortunate coincidences.

So eight years ago, we opened the doors of a foundation that enables givers to fund local ministries and charities as well as other organizations that feed, clothe, house, educate, and heal people all over the world. And we believe that God has absolutely blessed our efforts.

One more epiphany: One Saturday, while I was out working in the yard (You wouldn't believe what an exhilarating feeling it is to do manual labor when at one time you were physically unable to move.), I was thinking, *God, You gave me the awesome responsibility to build this foundation. How can I get the word out more efficiently than just through one-on-one contact? What should I do to promote the foundation?*

Then, I just waited ... listening.

No voice, just words came. "I don't want you to promote the foundation."

I thought, *What?*

He continued, "The foundation is only part of the picture. I want you to teach people about generosity. All people. Everybody."

On my end, a long period of thoughtful silence followed. This was something I had never considered. Not just Christians. *Everybody.*

What a concept, I thought. Not just "preaching to the

choir." This could be an outreach to everyone—all-inclusive—a movement that could really change the world. I was so excited I went in and told Nancy, who was just a little thrown off by my revelation. "O ... **kay,**" she said slowly, eyeing me, as if she was wondering if I'd suffered a heat stroke. "Uh ... weren't you just trimming the arborvitae?"

I told her again what had been communicated to me. "Well," she said, firmly this time, "okay. Whatever you need to do we'll do."

My first battle was won, as I knew we'd be doing whatever we needed to do together.

As I trimmed the overgrown bushes, my conversation continued. "You've been so generous to me. You created me, and You have given me everything that means anything to me. You have given me my wife, my children, our grandchildren, and our extended family. You have given me whatever talents and abilities I have. And You have given me absolutely everything else that I experience: the beauty of the earth, green grass, blue skies, clouds, trees, flowers, an incredible variety of animals, and the majesty of the universe as far as I can see; music and millions of voices in thousands of languages; the experiences of giving and receiving, of all of my senses, of being in community, and individual love. As a Christian, I know that You love me so much that You gave me the ultimate, most generous gift, the life of your son, Jesus Christ. In addition to all this, You continue to show Your love for me by giving me grace over and over and over again when I don't deserve it, including a second chance at life."

Second Chance

Now you know why we wrote this book. We believe that we've been called to take that next step outside of our comfort zone, not just to teach those Christians who might still be unaware of the need to model their Creator in His unparalleled generosity, but also to venture outside of our protected bubble to help all people of differing convictions understand their own generous roots and to help them convey their love to their fellow man through generosity.

Great journeys begin with an idea, which is followed by a step. Journeys of generosity are the same. A gift to another is a powerful thing in the universe. It can be small or large, a dollar to a homeless man or ten thousand dollars to an orphanage.

Remember the starfish. Remember that what you do can impact a life and that your help matters to that one. You possess that awesome power. It all starts with an idea, and you have plenty of them.

Alcorn, Randy. *The Treasure Principle: Unlocking the Secret of Joyful Giving*. Sisters: Multnomah Publishers, Inc., 2003.

Anwar, Yasmin. "Highly religious people are less motivated by compassion than are non-believers." UC Berkeley News Center, April 30, 2012.

Arrillaga-Andreessen, Laura. *Giving 2.0: Transform Your Giving and Our World*, San Francisco: Jossey-Bass, 2012.

Austin, Henry. "Muslims give more to charity than others, UK poll says" NBC News, http://www.nbcnews.com/news/other/muslims-give-more-charity-others-uk-poll-says-f6C10703224, July 22, 2013.

Barrett, David B. and Todd M Johnson. *World Christian Trends AD 30–AD 2000: Interpreting the Annual Christian Megacensus*. Pasadena: William Carey Library, 2001.

Barth, Glen. *The Good City: Transformed Lives Transforming Communities*. Tallmadge: S.D. Meyers Publishing Services, 2010.

Borgen, Clint. "The Cost to End World Hunger." The Borgen Project, http://borgenproject.org/the-cost-to-end-world-hunger/

Brafman, Ori and Rod A. Beckstrom. *The Starfish and the Spider: The Unstoppable Power of Leaderless Organizations*. New York: Penguin Group, 2006.

Brooks, Arthur C. *Gross National Happiness: Why Happiness Matters for America—and How We Can Get More of It*. New York: Basic Books, 2015.

Charities Aid Foundation. *World Giving Index 2013, A global view of giving trends*. Charities Aid Foundation, http://www.

cafonline.org/pdf/WorldGivingIndex2013_1374AWEB.pdf, 2014.

Clinton, Bill, *Giving: How Each of Us Can Change the World*, New York: Alfred A. Knopf, 2007.

Cole, Patrick. "Atheist Wilson Gives $22.5 Million for Catholic Fund." Bloomberg, http://www.morocco.com/forums/people-book-peuple-du-livre/26283-atheist-wilson-gives-22-5-million-catholic-fund.html#goto_threadtools, May 23, 2007.

Conway, Tom, Steve Gardner, William F High, Jerry Nuerge, Ryan Zeeb. *-un-Heritage, Eleven Pitfalls to Family Legacy and How to Avoid Them*. Fort Wayne: Center for Family Conversations, 2014.

Cox, Jeff. "15% of Americans on Food Stamps." CNBC, http://business.nbcnews.com/_news/2012/09/05/13682742-report-15-of-americans-on-food-stamps, September 5, 2012.

Crown Financial Ministries. *Money & Possession Scriptures*. Crown Financial Ministries, https://www.crownmoneymap.org/MoneyMap/SmallGroup/Downloads/2300ScriptureReferences_6_08.pdf, 2005.

Daniels, Alex. "Charities Try New Strategies as Fundraising Rebounds." *Chronicle of Philanthropy*, http://philanthropy.com/article/Charities-Try-New-Strategies/147167/, June 17, 2014.

Daniels, Alex and Anu Narayanswamy. "The Income-Inequality Divide Hits Generosity: Lower- and middle-class Americans give bigger share of income to charity than the richest in recession's wake." *Chronicle of Philanthropy*, http://philanthropy.com/article/The-Income-Inequality-Divide/149117/, October 5, 2014.

Dewan, Shaila. "An Ambiguous Omen, U.S. Household Debt Begins to Rise Again." *New York Times*, http://www.nytimes.com/2014/02/19/business/economy/an-ambiguous-omen-us-household-debt-begins-to-rise-again.html, February 18, 2014.

Donovan, Doug; Ben Gose, Maria Di Mento. "Gifts Surge From Rich U. S. Donors." *Chronicle of Philanthropy*, http://philanthropy.com/article/Gifts-Surge-From-Rich-U-S/144601/, February 9, 2014.

Dunn, Elizabeth and Michael Norton. *Happy Money: The Science of Smarter Spending.* New York: Simon & Schuster, 2013.

Ekins, Emily. "Americans Say Government Wastes Half of Every Tax Dollar it Collects," Reason-Rupe Poll, http://reason.com/poll/2014/04/11/americans-say-government-wastes-half-of, Apr. 11, 2014.

Elliott, Aaron. *In the Spirit of Nehemiah*, Aaron E. Elliott, 2012.

Enright, William. "Religious Giving: The Bumpy Ride Continues, Giving USA 2013." *Insights Newsletter*, Lake Institute on Faith & Giving, Lilly Family School of Philanthropy, Indiana University, Issue #2, http://www.philanthropy.iupui.edu/insights-newsletter, June 2013.

—"Giving USA 2012 Report." *Insights Newsletter,* Lake Institute on Faith & Giving, Lilly Family School of Philanthropy, Indiana University, Issue #2, http://www.philanthropy.iupui.edu/insights-newsletter, June 2012.

Firestone, Lisa, PhD. "Generosity — What's in it for You?" *Psychology Today*, http://www.psychologytoday.com/blog/compassion-matters/201011/generosity-what-s-in-it-you, November 24, 2010.

Fronsdal, Gil. *The Dhammapada: A New Translation of the Buddhist Classic with Annotations.* Boston: Shambhala, 2005.

Galvin, Beth. "A young boy comes to the aid of cash-strapped family." My Fox Atlanta, http://www.myfoxatlanta.com/story/20605651/young-boy-raises-60k-for-charities, January 16, 2013.

Gilbert, Matthew. "Self-help books and the promise of change." *Boston Globe*, http://www.bostonglobe.com/arts/books/2014/01/14/self-help-books-and-promise-change/4nJqRBpinOSWQ4wU536jPP/story.html?p1=Article_Facet_Related_Article, January 14, 2014.

Gipple, Emily and Ben Gose. "America's Generosity Divide." *Chronicle of Philanthropy*, http://philanthropy.com/article/ America-s-Generosity-Divide/133775/, August 19, 2012.

Global Health: Science and Progress, Human Trafficking, Sex Slavery, Bondage, http://www.ghspjournal.org/ content/2/3/261.full

Greve, Frank. "America's Poor Are its Most Generous Givers." *McClatchy Newspapers*, http://www.mcclatchydc. com/2009/05/19/68456_americas-poor-are-its-most- generous.html?rh=1, May 19, 2009.

Hall, Holly. "Donations Barely Grew at All Last Year, 'Giving USA' Finds." *Chronicle of Philanthropy*, http://philanthropy.com/ article/Donations-Barely-Grew-at-All/132367/?cid=pt, June 19, 2012.

Hansen, Mark Victor. "The Miracle of Tithing, Dedicated to tithers and future tithers everywhere." xehupatl.com, http:// www.brainybetty.com/2007Motivation/Markpercent20Vict orpercent20Hansenpercent20-percent20Thepercent20Mir aclepercent20ofpercent20Tithing.pdf

Harack, Ben. "How much would it cost to end extreme poverty in the world?" *Vision of Earth*, http://www.visionofearth. org/economics/ending-poverty/how-much-would-it-cost- to-end-extreme-poverty-in-the-world/, August 26, 2011.

Hrywna, Mark and Patrick Sullivan. "Donations More Than Doubled for Giving Tuesday." *Non Profit Times*, http://www. thenonprofittimes.com/news-articles/donations-more- than-doubled-for-giving-tuesday/, December 4, 2013.

Hurd, Rick. "Concord 'Mystery Man' gave away groceries to shake the blues." *Contra Costa Times*, http://www.mercurynews. com/my-town/ci_26196119/concord-mystery-man-gave- away-groceries-shake-blues, July 22, 2014.

Indiana University Lilly School of Philanthropy. *The Annual Report of Philanthropy for the Year 2013*. http://store. givingusareports.org/Giving-USA-2014-The-Annual-Report- on-Philanthropy-for-the-Year-2013-Digital-Package-P111. aspx, Giving USA 2014.

— *The Annual Report of Philanthropy for the Year 2012.* Giving USA 2013. http://store.givingusareports.org/Giving-USA-2013-The-Annual-Report-on-Philanthropy-for-the-Year-2012-Package-Digital-Edition-P99.aspx

— *The Annual Report of Philanthropy for the Year 2011.* http://store.givingusareports.org/Giving-USA-2012-The-Annual-Report-on-Philanthropy-for-the-Year-2011-Executive-Summary-P43.aspx, Giving USA 2012.

Jewish Publication Society. *JPS Hebrew-English Tanakh.* Philadelphia: Jewish Publication Society, 2000.

Johnson, Caitlin. "Cutting Through Advertising Clutter." CBS News, http://www.cbsnews.com/news/cutting-through-advertising-clutter/, September 17, 2006.

Johnson, Paul. *A History of the Jews.* New York: Harper & Row, 1988.

Jones, Jeffrey M. "Americans Say Federal Gov't Wastes Over Half of Every Dollar: Believe state and local governments waste proportionately less money," Gallup Poll News Service, http://www.highbeam.com/doc/1G1-268427080.html, September 19, 2011.

Keller, Gray, Dr. "Love: The Foundation of Philanthropy," *Beyond Money: A Look at Giving,* InternationalSolutions. BlogSpot.com, http://intentionalsolutions.blogspot.com/search?updated-max=2013-03-17T05:00:00-04:00&max-results=7&start=14&by-date=false, March 15, 2013.

Kelley, Matt. "Biden Gave an Average of $369 to charity a year." *USA Today,* http://usatoday30.usatoday.com/news/politics/election2008/2008-09-12-biden-financial_n.htm, September 12, 2008.

Kidder, Tracy. *Mountains Beyond Mountains: The Quest of Dr. Paul Farmer, a Man Who Would Cure the World.* New York: Random House, Inc., 2003.

Konrath, Sara. "Motives Matter: Why we volunteer has an impact on our health." University of Michigan Institute for Social Research, http://home.isr.umich.edu/releases/

motives-matter-why-we-volunteer-has-an-impact-on-our-health/, September 6, 2011

Kroll, Luisa. "Inside the 2013 Forbes 400: Facts And Figures On America's Richest." *Forbes,* http://www.forbes.com/sites/luisakroll/2013/09/16/inside-the-2013-forbes-400-facts-and-figures-on-americas-richest/, September 16, 2013.

Labarre, Polly. "How to Lead a Rich Life." *Fast Company,* http://www.fastcompany.com/46097/how-lead-rich-life, February 8, 2003.

Lao-Tse. *Tao Te-Ching.* Radford: Wilder Publications, 2009.

Lindsay, Jay, Associated Press. "Study Finds Less Religious States Give Less to Charity." *USA Today.* http://usatoday30.usatoday.com/news/religion/story/2012-08-20/religion-charity-study/57159760/1, August 2012.

Lopez, Donald. *Buddhist Scriptures.* New York: Penguin Classics, 2004.

MacLaughlin, Steve, Director. "Charitable Giving Report: How Nonprofit Fundraising Performed in 2013." Blackbaud Idea Lab, *https://www.blackbaud.com/files/resources/downloads/2014/2013.CharitableGivingReport.pdf,* 2014.

— Charitable Giving Report: "How Nonprofit Fundraising Performed in 2012." Blackbaud Idea Lab, https://www.blackbaud.com/files/resources/downloads/2012.CharitableGivingReport.pdf, 2013.

Maulana, Muhammad Ali. *The Holy Quar'an with English Translation and Commentary.* Dublin: Ahmadiyya Anjuman Isha'at Islam Lahore Inc., USA, 2002.

May, Caroline. "Level of volunteerism in America hits record low." *Daily Caller,* http://dailycaller.com/2014/03/03/level-of-volunteerism-in-america-hits-record-low/, March 3, 2014.

McGowan Dale. *Parenting Beyond Belief, On Raising Ethical, Caring Kids Without Religion.* New York: ANACOM, 2007.

Mitchell, Stephen. *Bagvadh Gita, A New Translation.* New York: Harper Collins, 1988.

Moll, Jorge; Frank Krueger, Ronald Zahn, Matteo Pardini, Ricardo de Oliveria-Souza, Jordan Grafman. "Human fronto-mesolimbic networks guide decisions about charitable donation." Proceedings of the National Academy of Sciences of the United States of America, http://www.pnas.org/content/103/42/15623.full, October 9, 2006.

Moses - John of Patmos. *The Holy Bible, New International Version*. Grand Rapids: Zondervan Corporation, 1973, 1978, 1984.

Nyl, Steven. "Hoarders, Storage Wars, and Lenten observances." *Generosity Monk*, http://generositymonk.com/w/2014/03/18/5763/, March 18, 2014.

Pew Research. "'Nones' on the Rise." Pew Research Religion & Public Life Project, http://www.pewforum.org/2012/10/09/nones-on-the-rise/, October 9, 2012.

Research and Statistics Group. "Quarterly Report on Household Debt and Credit." Federal Reserve Bank of New York, Microeconomic Studies, http://www.newyorkfed.org/householdcredit/2013-Q3/HHDC_2013Q3.pdf, November 2013.

Ryan, M. J. *The Giving Heart: Unlocking the Transformative Power of Generosity in Your Life*. Berkeley: Conari Press, 2000.

Saad, Lydia. "U.S., Rise in Religious 'Nones' Slows in 2012." Gallup Poll, http://www.gallup.com/poll/159785/rise-religious-nones-slows-2012.aspx, 2012.

Sachs, Jeffrey. *The End of Poverty: Economic Possibilities for Our Time*, New York: Penguin Group, 2005.

Schaarsmith, Amy McConnell. "Shoe-shining benefactor to Children's Hospital to retire after 30 years." *Pittsburgh Post-Gazette*, http://www.post-gazette.com/local/city/2013/12/17/Hanging-up-his-boots/stories/201312170082, December 17, 2013.

Seuss, Dr. *How the Grinch Stole Christmas!* New York: Random House, 1957.

Shah, Neil. "U.S. Household Net Worth Hits Record High, Surging Stock Market and Rising Home Values Deliver Benefits, Especially for Affluent." *Wall Street Journal,* http://online.wsj.com/news/articles/SB10001424052702303824204579423183397213204, March 6, 2014.

Smith, Christian and Hilary Davidson. *The Paradox of Generosity, Giving We Receive, Grasping We Lose*: Oxford Press, NY, NY, 2014.

Solomon, Norman. *The Talmud: A Selection*. New York: Penguin Classics, 2009.

Staff. "Daily Livestock Report." CME Group, Vol. 9, No. 243,, http://www.dailylivestockreport.com/documents/dlrpercent2012-20-2011.pdf, December 20, 2011.

Staff. "Fast facts — consumption statistics." *Green Living Tips*, http://www.greenlivingtips.com/articles/consumption-statistics.html, May 4th, 2012.

Staff. "Forbes: The 400 Richest People in America," *Forbes*, September 20, 2012.

Staff. "Market Trends, Composition and Crowdfunding Platforms.a Crowdfunding Industry Report," http://www.crowdsourcing.org/document/crowdfunding-industry-report-market-trends-composition-and-crowdfunding-platforms/14277, May 2012.

Staff. "Price of Safe Water for All: $10 Billion and the Will to Provide It," *New York Times*, http://www.nytimes.com/2000/11/23/world/price-of-safe-water-for-all-10-billion-and-the-will-to-provide-it.html, November 23, 2000.

Staff. "Rich or poor, giving makes you happy: global research finds rare evidence of universal trait," *UBC News*, May 9, 2013.

Staff. "Thinking About Giving, Not Receiving, Motivates People to Help Others." Association for Psychological Science, http://www.psychologicalscience.org/index.php/news/releases/thinking-about-giving-not-receiving-motivates-people-to-help-others.html, August 9, 2012.

Staff. "Towards the end of poverty." *The Economist*, http://www.economist.com/news/leaders/21578665-nearly-1-billion-people-have-been-taken-out-extreme-poverty-20-years-world-should-aim, June 1, 2013.

Stearns, Richard. *The Hole in Our Gospel: What Does God Expect of Us? The Answer That Changed My Life and Might Just Change the World*. Nashville: W Publishing, 2014.

Stern, Ken. "Why the Rich Don't Give to Charity." *Atlantic*, http://www.theatlantic.com/magazine/archive/2013/04/why-the-rich-dont-give/309254/, March 20, 2013.

Story, Louise. "Anywhere the Eye Can See, It's Likely to See an Ad." *New York Times*, http://www.nytimes.com/2007/01/15/business/media/15everywhere.html?pagewanted=all&_r=0, January 15, 2007.

Sullivan, Missy. "Lost Inheritance: Studies show Americans blow through family fortunes at a remarkable rate. With trillions being passed on, can today's baby boomers break the cycle?" *Wall Street Journal*, http://www.wsj.com/articles/SB10001424127887324662404578334663271139552, March 8, 2013.

Svoboda, Elizabeth. "Scientists Are Finding That We Are Hard-Wired for Giving," Science of Generosity, Exploring an Essential Human Virtue, University of Notre Dame, http://generosityresearch.nd.edu/news/42488-hard-wired-for-giving/, September 5, 2013.

Swanson, Eric and Sam Williams. *To Transform a City: Whole Church, Whole Gospel, Whole City*. Grand Rapids: Zondervan, 2010.

Sweeney, Chip. *A New Kind of Big: How Churches of Any Size Can Transform Their Communities*. Grand Rapids: Baker Books, 2011.

TABLE: "A Look at the 50 Most Generous Donors of 2012." *Chronicle of Philanthropy*, http://philanthropy.com/article/Table-The-50-Most-Generous/137245/, February 3, 2013.

Tehmee. "The Average American is exposed to 3000 Adverts per day ..." MarketingFanaticism.wordpress.com, http://marketingfanaticism.wordpress.com/2012/02/24/the-average-american-is-exposed-to-3000-adverts-per-day/, February 24, 2012.

Tsvetkova, Milena and Michael Macy. "The Science of 'Paying It Forward'." *New York Times Sunday Review*, http://www.

nytimes.com/2014/03/16/opinion/sunday/the-science-of-paying-it-forward.html, March 14, 2014.

Tuttle, Hudson. *The Ethics of Spiritualism: System of Moral Philosophy, Founded on Evolution and the Continuity of Man's Existence Beyond the Grave*. 1878.

Van Note, Vanessa. "The Whole You: Domino Effect," *Independent Florida Alligator*, http://m.alligator.org/blogs/wednesday/article_fa245cde-1d1b-11e4-9b08-0019bb2963f4.html?mode=jqm, August 6, 2014.

Varda. *Hebrew - English Torah, the Five Books of Moses*. Skokie: Varda Books, 2012.

Velasco, Schuyler. "Black Friday weekend sales disappoint. Can retailers recover?" *Christian Science Monitor*, http://www.csmonitor.com/Business/2013/1202/Black-Friday-weekend-sales-disappoint.-Can-retailers-recover-video, December 2, 2013.

Video. "GOOD: Get Your Volunteer On." *GOOD Magazine*, YouTube, https://www.youtube.com/watch?v=W7xmCQgDxnk, November 18, 2008.

Wikipedia. iHistory of Wikipedia.i *Wikipedia*, http://en.wikipedia.org/wiki/History_of_Wikipedia, February 15, 2014.

Wilson, Andrew. *World Scripture, a Comparative Anthology of Sacred Texts*. St. Paul: Paragon House, September 22, 1998.

Wolfman-Arent, Avi and Cody Switzer. "Chart: Gifts From Ice-Bucket Challenge Exceed $100-Million." *Chronicle of Philanthropy*, http://philanthropy.com/article/Chart-Gifts-From-Ice-Bucket/148457/, August 29, 2014.

Wright, Lauren Tyler. *Giving: The Sacred Art: Creating a Lifestyle of Generosity*. Woodstock: SkyLights Paths Publishing, 2008.

Additional Resources

- American Humanist Association
- Citizens Against Government Waste
- Faith and Service Technical Education Network (FASTEN)
- Fidelity Charitable
- Generous Giving
- Global Issues
- GlobalRichList.com
- Jewish Communal Fund
- Justice Ventures International
- National Alliance to End Homelessness
- National Center for Missing and Exploited Children, The
- National Christian Foundation
- National Coalition for the Homeless
- National Law Center for Homelessness and Poverty
- National Underground Railroad Freedom Center
- Schwab Donor Advised Fund
- Shared Hope International
- Unitarian Universalist Association
- United Nations World Food Programme
- United Way
- US National Debt Clock
- Vanguard
- World Health Organization
- World Hunger Education Service
- World Water Council

INDEX

Printed in the United States
By Bookmasters